Motherhood changes work-outside-the-home mothers in ways that are hard to put into words. Yet if anyone has beautifully captured the *before* and *after* of a career "detoured" by family, it's Jen Babakhan. Has your plan for the perfect work/family balance fallen apart? Are you plagued by worries that you'll lose yourself as you pour out your life for others? Jen understands. With tender confessions and hope-filled encouragement, Jen's words will be a soothing balm to your soul. She reminds all of us moms that the truth of God's provision and care for us—and our kids—is something we can depend on. Through these pages you'll discover the joy of living the fullness God intended. It's a wonderful book, and I already have a list of friends I'm eager to share it with!

—**Tricia Goyer,** mom of ten and *USA Today* bestselling author of 70+ books, including *Calming Angry Kids*

This is the book I wish I would have had when I left behind a news career in the city to become a stay-at-home mom on the farm. I've never regretted that decision, but I desperately needed the peace and contentment that Jen holds out to moms in her debut book, *Detoured.* With personal insights and helpful advice, this book beautifully celebrates the gift of motherhood.

—**Jennifer Dukes Lee,** author of *It's All Under Control* and *The Happiness Dare*

Jen Babakhan has a life-changing message for anyone who has ever found herself experiencing an unexpected detour in life. Filled with audacious honesty, practical ideas, and deep wisdom, this is the kind of book that will help you regain your perspective and get unstuck from the false beliefs that are holding you back.

—**Mandy Arioto,** president and CEO, MOPS International

DETOURED

JEN BABAKHAN

HARVEST HOUSE PUBLISHERS
EUGENE, OREGON

Cover design by Connie Gabbert Design + Illustration

Cover photo © philia / Shutterstock

Published in association with Books & Such Literary Management, 52 Mission Circle, Suite 122, PMB 170, Santa Rosa, CA 95409-5370, www.booksandsuch.com.

Detoured
Copyright © 2019 by Jen Babakhan
Published by Harvest House Publishers
Eugene, Oregon 97408
www.harvesthousepublishers.com

ISBN 978-0-7369-7673-2 (pbk.)
ISBN 978-0-7369-7674-9 (eBook)

Library of Congress Cataloging-in-Publication Data

Names: Babakhan, Jen, 1981- author.
Title: Detoured / Jen Babakhan.
Description: Eugene : Harvest House Publishers, 2019.
Identifiers: LCCN 2019004513 (print) | LCCN 2019008939 (ebook) | ISBN 9780736976749 (ebook) | ISBN 9780736976732 (pbk.)
Subjects: LCSH: Mothers--Religious life. | Motherhood--Religious aspects--Christianity. | Vocation--Christianity. | Identity (Psychology)--Religious aspects--Christianity. | Change (Psychology)--Religious aspects--Christianity.
Classification: LCC BV4529.18 (ebook) | LCC BV4529.18 .B32 2019 (print) | DDC 248.8/431--dc23
LC record available at https://lccn.loc.gov/2019004513

Printed in the United States of America

19 20 21 22 23 24 25 26 27 / BP-AR / 10 9 8 7 6 5 4 3 2 1

For Ed, Bryce, and Bradley

You are evidence of how extravagantly God loves me,
and this book is as much yours as mine.
I'll love you forever.

Contents

Release and Surrender

Everyone loves good *before* and *after* photos. Before and after *what* really doesn't matter as long as there's a visible difference between the two. Typically, the *after* photo shows a drastic improvement of some sort. When I think about what my own photos would look like, however, this would be reversed. Imagine this with me: In my *before*, I'm wearing a lavender dress shirt tucked into charcoal gray dress pants. My dark hair is carefully pulled up, with just enough kept out to frame my face. My face is freshly made up, and my pearl earrings match my necklace. I'm on a business trip with colleagues, and I'm vibrant. Surrounded by work-friends I've known for years, I'm enjoying laughter and conversation.

In my *after*, I'm wearing charcoal lounge pants with a limp drawstring, paired with a fitted blue T-shirt from Target. My dark hair is peppered with rogue grays refusing to lie flat, and it is pulled into a messy ponytail. My face is naked, and I'm wearing no accessories. I'm a mother of two and, by the looks of it, exhausted. I'm alone with my infant son asleep on my chest, scrolling through my Facebook feed to numb the loneliness.

My *before* and *after* images are clearly different, but one thing—the most important thing—remains unchanged. Dressed up or down, working professional or professional baby-rocker, my worth in Christ remains untouched.

Do you feel like your worse-than-before *after* photo is permanent? Like, when you traded career for kids, you actually traded in your identity? I promise you, neither of those is true. When I began writing this book (in between diaper changes, endless snack serving, and Target runs), I held the vision of you in mind—and my prayer was that this book would help you blend your *before* and *after* photos into an image that accurately reflects the truth of who you are in Christ. Transition is hard. Being home with children all day long is exhausting. I know you're tempted to settle for a life of sweatpants, Internet surfing, and missing your work-friends (or maybe just drinking coffee in silence), but Jesus wants more for us. We still have purpose. The world still needs us. We never relinquished our most important title: Daughter of God.

If you're holding this book in your hands, then you've done the miraculous thing that is taking time for yourself. You might feel guilty about this simple act (you probably do). Take a deep breath and know that you are not alone. You aren't alone in the endless laundry, the yelling, the crying because you yelled, or the hopelessness that is born of daily monotony. This isn't the life you planned or imagined when you walked away from your career and toward the family you love even more. I know that the loneliness you feel is isolating and deafening. Motherhood is the constant pouring out of yourself that threatens to leave you empty, asking you at times to give up more than you feel like you're getting.

Following God's call to surrender my career felt a lot like giving up my identity. Many of my friends and those closest to me disappeared in the process, an unanticipated loss that shook my confidence. At the end of each day at home with my newborn son, I mourned the loss of a sense of accomplishment. The dishes were done, the baby was changed—but what difference did that make in the *real* world? I had confused my work with my worth, though

I couldn't see it at the time. It's a mistake many of us have made. If you're like me, letting go of your career to stay home with your children brought joy but also unexpected grief and a sense of loss.

This book is for you. Motherhood doesn't offer performance evaluations or a pat on the back for a job well done. Instead of talking about current events in the break room, you're making lunch and building Legos with your little colleagues. I'm guessing you might feel a bit overqualified for your current position. But God has been preparing you for this season all along.

This doesn't mean that letting go of a professional title and embracing this calling to be home with your children will be—or has been—easy or painless. Growing pains are inevitable. It's a process that includes acknowledging some false beliefs you might not realize you've subscribed to and releasing your white-knuckle grip on control. Only in this release and true surrender will you have the ability to understand that your worth has nothing to do with your achievements. You are not what you do.

You are not what you do.

My hope and prayer is that when you finish the last page of this book, you see yourself not as a *before* or *after* image, but as a woman *becoming*. Although you may feel like you've left behind meaningful work, I assure you: Much still lies before you. Thank you for joining me on this path with the perhaps unforeseen detour. Let's not forget, sometimes the unexpected paths are the most beautiful.

Having It All Isn't the Goal

The Lie We All Believe

For everything there is a season; a time
for every activity under heaven.

Ecclesiastes 3:1 (NLT)

In the fall of 2011, I stood in front of a classroom full of parents. I was eight months pregnant, glistening with sweat (I appreciated those who lied and said I was glowing), and breathlessly gave my Back-to-School Night parent information speech. I told the parents listening intently that I would eagerly return to finish the year as their child's third-grade teacher. I had every intention of returning to work in a few short months. I was determined to do the exact thing I had seen countless colleagues do: prepare a long-term substitute to teach my class, have the baby, learn how to do the mothering thing well, and drop the baby off with a sitter. Like a well-executed lesson plan, life with baby would fall into place seamlessly because I was prepared.

As the parents filed out of my classroom that night, one of the mothers hesitated in the doorway. She looked into my eyes, her own shining with tears, and said, "Please take all the time you can with your baby. You will never have this time back." She patted my shoulder and wished me well, and I felt conflicted in a way I hadn't before. I brushed off her comment and told myself I was making too much of it. My colleagues came back to work after maternity leave tired and tearful, but they did it. Their classrooms continued to run like well-oiled machines, and they didn't miss a beat. I would do the same.

My son Bryce was born in the wee hours of a September morning, blue and breathless, and given to a waiting respiratory team in the delivery room. It felt like a year passed in the few seconds it took him to take his first breath, but when he did, the entire room let out cheers of joy. In that moment, as I watched his purple-tinged toes turn pink, I felt indescribable joy for the first time in my life. I was a Mother. It felt like the title I was born to hold.

In the sleep-deprived days that followed, I continuously tried to make myself comfortable with the fact that I was going to eventually leave my son and return to my classroom. As I held Bryce, sleeping against my chest just hours after his birth, I turned to my husband, Ed, and said, "I'm not going back to work." I said it knowing that we could never afford for me to quit my job, but I needed to say the words that my soul would not stop whispering. Ed chuckled and responded, "Okay. You will eventually, though, right?" I'm still grateful that he responded so graciously and without expressing any fear about our finances. He wanted me to be home with our son, too, as impossible as it felt financially.

Before I had Bryce, my image of a stay-at-home mother was June

Cleaver. She baked cookies and cleaned, and her children always behaved and left her alone to bake cookies and clean. I didn't want that for myself. Prior to teaching I worked in marketing and frequently traveled the country for business. I loved the excitement of seeing new places, flying into new airports, and having hotel rooms all to myself. I had worked hard to get my college degree. I loved dressing professionally, going to upscale work events, and handing out business cards with my name on them. I made the career change to become a teacher when traveling lost its luster and I no longer felt inspired by the work I was doing. As a child, I'd dreamed of being a teacher, and I felt God calling me to the classroom. And so I went. In 2007 I did the unthinkable and quit my incredibly secure job to enter the budget-impaired field of public education.

It took me a year to get hired, and two years later I earned my permanent status in the district. I loved teaching. I loved decorating my classroom and watching struggling students learn how to multiply and read. It felt amazing when parents asked me for advice about how to help their child at home. I felt knowledgeable. Competent. I felt important.

The year I earned my long-awaited tenure was also the year I resigned.

What Happens When You're Forced Off the Fence

I struggled to make sense of my decision. I shouldn't have been so surprised that life would throw a curveball when I least expected.

Two years before, I had rescued a German shepherd puppy from a man who seemingly appeared out of nowhere. "Hey, you want a dog?" he yelled above the din of the midafternoon traffic.

When I heard him shouting, I was running along the side of

the road chasing a small dog that had nearly been hit by a car. Driving home from school, I pulled to the side of the road to try to help the dog find its owner. That's when the man appeared and asked if I would rescue the puppy he held in his arms, the puppy that he no longer wanted. He held up a three-pound ball of shivering fluff that I instantly agreed to take home and convince Ed we needed to keep.

I can still remember the feeling of her muddy paws soaking through my jeans on the way home as I thought of all the ways I could plead her case to stay with us. When Ed saw the adorable pup, he instantly agreed to keep her, and we jointly decided to table any plans of having children. We had been on the fence about having kids for a while, and we frequently waffled back and forth between adopting a dog and having a baby. *Were we cut out to be good parents? Did we have what it would take to raise a child?* My personal fear of carrying a child reflected my own doubt in my ability to handle a pregnancy and the morning sickness that was sure to come with it. *How would I go to work every day sick?* Having a baby right now seemed inconvenient at best and, at worst, impossible. Surely, the arrival of the dog in our lives was a sign we were meant to have a dog and not a baby.

We spent the next weekend purchasing every kind of puppy product we could find at the local pet supply store—even though I felt a nagging sense that we had chosen wrong. *Was a puppy truly the right decision? It* had *to be*, I reasoned with myself. *We had a new puppy!* Why couldn't I silence the soft voice within that told me motherhood was a risk worth taking?

Two days later God proved Himself faithful to answer: My shaking hand held a positive pregnancy test, and my heart held wonder and disbelief. We had chosen wrong. God, in His infinite mercy, gave us the chance to experience both options simultaneously so that we would know what our hearts—and what He—really desired for our lives. I realized then that my own fears of becoming pregnant (and nauseated constantly) left no room for the work and provision of Christ in my life.

> *My fears left no room for the work and*
> *provision of Christ in my life.*

I had forgotten that the God I serve was intimately aware of my fear—and abundantly equipped to resolve it. We were able to find the puppy a wonderful home (I knew my limits, and training a puppy and having a baby at the same time were beyond them), and I knew that my pregnancy was a gift beyond measure.

Yet, two years and a baby later, none of my life made sense. I was finally going to have it all, the way I thought God intended, and yet I felt as though my plan for the perfect life was falling apart. I made it through my pregnancy without vomiting in front of my third-grade students (a miracle in itself), and I survived labor and childbirth. *Wasn't that enough challenging of the false beliefs I held about God?* Three months after I gave birth, my newborn baby began bleeding internally due to a sensitivity to milk protein. After appointments with pediatric allergists and specialists, it became clear that Bryce's diet (and mine, since I breastfed) would require close supervision and that healing would take place over a period of months.

> *My plan for the perfect life*
> *was falling apart.*

My infant son had a severe dairy intolerance that required me to be home with him. The choice between working and staying home with Bryce was no longer mine to make. Ed and I would have to find a way to make it work financially. And yet I still went in circles in my mind. *Was this truly what I was meant to do? Did I come this far professionally only to give it all up? And I just got tenure! Who does this? Besides, my students and their parents expected me to return to work, as I had emphatically promised I would.* So much had changed since I had last stood in front of them...

Then came the guilt. The arrival of motherhood brought with it a love for my child so intense I couldn't fathom my heart or body being big enough to contain it all. From the very moment I laid eyes on Bryce's face—swollen and wrinkly from delivery—I knew that the love washing over me was different from any I'd ever felt. *If I loved my son so much, why was I struggling with this?* Bryce needed me, and he was my top priority now—not my work, my goals, or my dreams. Could it really be that God was again asking me to trust His strength instead of my own?

For so many of us, the choice between working outside of the home and staying home with our children was made for us. Perhaps your child has a health condition that requires you to be home, or maybe you simply cannot afford daycare so you quit your job. Before I became pregnant with my first son, I often told my coworkers that if I ever had a child, I would want to stay home. I said it in passing, often after a frustrating day of pouring myself into other people's children. Why wouldn't I want to offer all of me to my own?

And yet when it came time to actually stay home with my son, the choice was more difficult than I had anticipated. I can remember the exact moment I signed my letter of resignation. Emotions flooded me, all of them funneled into the checkmark I made in a box next to the words stating I would not return to work the following school year. Tears filled my eyes as, conflicted, I breathed a sigh of relief. I felt as though I was finally free of so many burdens and worries that had filled my mind in the months leading up to the decision. I was finally on an endless summer vacation with my sweet son, and it felt too good to be true.

As soon as I allowed my mind to venture into the unfettered joy of following God's direction, I heard the negative voice I knew too well begin to weigh in. *What if you just made a huge mistake?* it whispered. In that moment, I reminded myself I hadn't and brushed it off. *I can always go back when Bryce is older*, I consoled myself. I glanced over at my boy, playing quietly by himself, oblivious to what felt like a life-changing moment for Mom, and knew I had made the right decision. I was meant to be home with him, and I *wanted* to be. Even though I knew being home was both right and what I wanted, I could never have predicted the emotional tidal wave that would wash over me the following two years.

All of our stories are different, but we have all believed the same lie—that it is possible to "have it all." We believe that not only is it possible, but that lots of other women have found the secret to having it all. We look at our neighbors, friends, even women in the grocery store and think, *She's got it together.* The biggest lie, however, is that we should want it all. We accept the idea that, in order to live complete lives, we need full-to-the-brim social, work, and home lives, with the right balance of "me" time—and all of this documented on social media. Yet our children clamor for 99.8 percent of our attention, and we feel guilty for being overwhelmed. If all of the social events, careers, family, and friends were stripped away, who would we even be?

If the social events, careers, family, and friends were stripped away, who would we even be?

Can I tell you a secret? "Having it all" is not the goal. The first moment I held Bryce, heaven still fresh on his breath, I knew that it wasn't. In that hospital room, silent and still after the chaos of birth, I felt my world tilt on its axis. No longer was I concerned about lessons or e-mails; none of that mattered anymore. *This,* I felt Jesus whisper to my soul. *This is what life really is—here in your arms.* I could sit and weep as I remember those early moments in that dimly lit hospital room when I felt as though heaven had revealed itself to me in an instant. Sirens blared in the distance as ambulances pulled into the emergency bay of the hospital, and there I sat in serenity, embracing new life and all it now held for me.

The secret to fulfillment isn't striving to have it all. It never has been. When we can rest in our security as children of God, we are given extraordinary freedom to enjoy the moments that make up a life. No longer are we slaves to striving and competing for the best God has to offer—because we are certain it is already ours.

I don't believe that God wants us to frantically flit from one thing to another, never pausing to inhale the delight of the present...and exhale gratitude for His gifts. He wants us to be here, in this moment, and grateful. The present is the only place we can truly sit with God. We can't follow Him anywhere else.

When I was knee-deep in new motherhood, I couldn't see past the next minute. During my pregnancy I read every book about babies I could get my hands on. I read about getting a baby to nurse correctly, to sleep correctly, and to calm down correctly. I was so intent on getting it right that I overlooked that whole "babies are actually tiny and unique humans" thing. Somehow it escaped me as a new mother that, once I actually had a baby in my arms, I might have some opinions and thoughts about what *my* individual child needed. As I held Bryce in my arms, not the hypothetical picture of a baby, the books and information became irrelevant.

Motherhood looked different—it *felt* different—from what I expected. All I knew was that my newborn son needed to be nursed every eight minutes (not the two hours the baby books promised), and I never understood how desperately a human needs sleep until I had not gotten more than thirty minutes in a row for days on end.

June Cleaver was nowhere to be found, and I was convinced that making cookies or cleaning would never happen in my house again. Nothing in my life was recognizable anymore, and I couldn't understand why I wasn't happy. My baby was healthy, and so was I. Was that not enough for me? I had so much to be thankful for, and the guilt I felt because of my lack of appreciation threatened to consume any ounce of joy I allowed myself to feel. *You're* home *while the rest of the world has to work. Your life is so easy. You don't deserve any of this. Take a walk! Vacuum again—do* something! I would chide myself.

If my day wasn't filled with activities that were meaningful and enriching to my baby, clearly I was failing in every way. I was letting God down. Being present in the moment felt both uncomfortable and like too much work. I hated being alone with my thoughts. Like an athlete who began a race before warming up, my mind would catapult to the future: I was always wondering when I would find the peace I craved—and skipping the important work of being still before God. As the months after I resigned continued on, my depression felt as though it came from an unexpected place. I was ashamed to admit what it was, so I threw all my energy into being the best stay-at-home mother I could possibly be. In between nursing for the umpteenth time, changing diapers, and giving my son his allotted ten minutes of "tummy time" every few hours, I cleaned like my hair was on fire. No dish ever sat in the sink, the floors were mopped every Monday, and the laundry was always done (never put away, though; I wasn't *that* crazy).

I was on my phone, scrolling through my Facebook feed, whenever I had the chance. While the baby nursed, I scrolled, endlessly, through image after image of other women, other moms, old coworkers who had it all. And I wondered, *Why wasn't I able to do it? What didn't I have that everyone else had? Why had the desire to be home with my child been placed so heavily on my chest that I couldn't breathe when I thought about returning to work?* I could not understand why such an easy decision was also the most difficult.

What I didn't recognize within myself was the deeply embedded belief that if others experienced success, there wouldn't be any left over for me. The coworkers who continued to work, achieving Teacher of the Year nominations and earning higher-level credentials, were not taking away my ability to one day do the same. Their success did not ensure my failure. God was asking me to turn my eyes to Him, not to the gifts He had given others. My heart fought with my head. My head fought with God. And His answer was clear whether or not I wanted to hear it: I was to stay home. My son needed me. My colleagues were on a different path. I heard God's gentle but firm voice in my heart. And it hurt.

While I—with tear-filled eyes—told my supervising principal about my dilemma, Bryce babbled happily atop the round meeting table. I had sat there so many times before to discuss students' growth or achievements. Al was already one of my favorite principals, someone many of us teachers looked to for guidance from his wealth of experience in the classroom.

"My wife took some time off, too, when our boys were little," he said, his eyes sparkling. "She taught, too, but spent those years at home with them, and it was wonderful."

I instantly felt my tears recede, and the lump in my throat grew smaller. Hearing him confirm that my decision to leave the classroom, for at least a little while, was a good one—or at least not unheard of—was a welcome change from the noise in my head that said I was making a bad career choice and that I'd never recover whatever I was sure to lose. I can see now that the voices I battled internally fed off my fear.

I still battle the voices sometimes. Now they tell me that if and when I return to work, I'll be too outdated and less knowledgeable than my coworkers. Maybe you sometimes feel the same. While the world of our fellow professionals keeps spinning, and the promotions roll in for those we once stood shoulder-to-shoulder with, our lives at home can feel suspended in time. We are moving for sure. In fact, it feels like we never sit still! But are we getting anywhere? The answer, of course, is that we certainly are. In these days of mundane kid chaos at home, our worlds are spinning faster than we realize.

In these days of mundane kid chaos at home, our worlds are spinning faster than we realize.

The speed at which our kids grow up is one of the many reasons it's vital for you to have something that is only yours and ignites a passion within you. At some point, your children will no longer need you in the same way they do now, and it's important you don't look to them for your own fulfillment. Only Christ can give us the kind of soul-fullness we seek, and we are made to embrace the abundance He offers us in all areas of life. (More on that later.)

Perhaps you question how you'll ever compete with the fresh-faced college graduates who know the latest buzzwords to use in an interview. In the end, it's all fear—and fear leaves no room for the One who came to conquer fear to work.

The woman described in Proverbs 31 comes to mind. She's often referred to as the virtuous woman, and the writer described in great detail her many admirable qualities. She's the epitome of a good wife and mother, and she tends to her family and their faith with great care. Verse 25 reads, "She is clothed with strength and dignity, and she laughs without fear of the future." We don't need to fear the future because God is already there—and when we trust Him, we can rejoice in the present as well as the future.

The moment you're living right now was the future at some point, and it was planned by your heavenly Father with your very best in mind. We can trust Him to take care of all of our days— even when we cannot imagine how they might look. Your life and all of its ordinary details are in His hands. He is more than capable of handling your future according to His purpose...if you let Him.

Raising two boys often feels like being a visitor in a foreign country. The world of my boys is often filled with the seemingly constant need to assess who is winning and losing in everything from getting in the car the fastest to putting toothpaste on their toothbrush before bed. I'm constantly hearing these words come out of my mouth: "It's not a competition." The thing is, for a long time I didn't believe my own words, and sometimes I still struggle with them.

Life is not a competition, but when you see your peers achieving things you once planned for yourself, it can sting a little (a lot) and feel like a competition that you're losing. Perhaps you hear through the grapevine that the coworker you used to chat with over coffee is promoted to vice president or makes partner. On the outside you're excited and congratulating her, but inwardly you're battling the jealousy you deny you harbor.

The belief that the success of others ensures our own failure is so deeply embedded in our culture that it's almost expected that envy or jealousy of others will arrive with the delivery of positive news. Engagements, pregnancy announcements, and weddings all bring out similar emotions and thoughts that we'd rather deny we experience. Think back to the years prior to getting married or having kids. Every time a friend of yours announced her engagement or pregnancy, I'm willing to bet that, deep down, you felt as though her good news somehow meant that these things were now less possible for you.

It might have been sheer disappointment that God's timing for your friend was not the same as His for you. While these emotions are valid—and I don't think we need to shame ourselves for any emotion—we do need to fact-check them to avoid being swept away by a wave of jealousy or disappointment. We have to be willing to become aware of our own false beliefs and unfounded thought patterns so that our response to other people's good news is genuine and loving. We know there is no shortage of good gifts from God.

When God calls us to something, there is no promise of painless transition. Following Him will cost us, and pain will be involved. Motherhood is a sacrifice in itself. We give our bodies over to join with the Creator in the act of creation, with the hope of a great reward for our offering. For some of you, this process was filled with heartache and dashed hopes. Having a child became something you not only dreamed about, but also placed on a pedestal built of high expectations and sheer determination to feel joyful regardless of your reality. If you fall in that category and having a baby didn't come easily, giving yourself the permission to admit you don't always enjoy motherhood without also feeling shame can be close to impossible. Motherhood isn't easy for any of us regardless of how we entered into it.

The challenge is not only the emotional fortitude that motherhood requires. We give of our physical and mental strength as we tirelessly care for our children, bending but not breaking, over and over again. How many nights have you gone to bed with an aching back after holding a sleeping baby for much of the day? Even if your children are no longer in the infant stage, I'm sure you can recall the feeling.

After our babies grow into toddlers, the exquisite maternal joys are peppered more often with frustrations we hesitate to speak aloud lest we be seen as imperfect mothers. The moments of wonder, cradling tiny feet in our hands, are replaced with exasperated sighs when food is thrown and tiny tempers flare. We recall so easily when our hearts were beautifully broken with love in the first breathtaking moments after birth, and we struggle to recover this same emotion.

That was the motherhood we signed up for. This one, with the toddler and his clenched fists of fury, is not. This is the beautiful breaking down, the relentless turning inside out, that is motherhood, with all of its joy and imperfection. It is ever-changing and consistently humbling. If our footing is not secure on the unshakable foundation of Jesus, we are easily lost in a sea of shifting emotion, constantly searching for shore. Our emotions are many things, but accurate gauges of our mothering ability or of our value, they are not.

Some things are so sacred, so holy, that they deserve our unwavering attention. Our worth in Christ, especially if we are unaware of it, is one of those things. When God sees that we need a refresher course in what we mean to Him and who we are in Him, He will ensure we get it. Now, in this new chapter of your life's story, you are letting go of what was once the trophy in your hand. The thing that declared to the world you were worthy, strong, and qualified. Your career or professional life is on the back burner, and you have a new journey to walk with God. He's asking you to stop striving for approval and achievement and to place your trust in who He says you are: worthy, righteous, beloved. These are the only titles your soul has truly ever held. His credentials are the only ones you need. You are anchored in Christ.

Our worth in Christ is a truth
so sacred, so holy, that it deserves
our unwavering attention.

When Achievement Becomes a Slippery Slope

I can remember the first time I felt the warm rush of adrenaline from an achievement. My parents and I were visiting my paternal grandparents and had just finished eating my grandmother's incredible fried chicken for dinner. We sat at the shiny wooden table in their kitchen, a large window on one side, and, on the other, a yellow clock shaped like an apple that ticked loudly whenever the room grew silent.

My Grandmother Alice's kitchen was a place of good food and even better memories, and as a little girl I loved nothing more than knowing there were *always* homemade cookies in the cookie jar sitting atop her oak china cabinet. Sitting around the table were aunts and uncles as well, and I was the only child there. I was around eight at the time, and I loved to read. I voraciously read anything I could find: cereal boxes at breakfast, magazines, and any book that happened to be lying within eyesight.

My mother was proud of my reading ability that exceeded my grade level, and she often beamed with pride as she told others about the books I was able to read. When the conversation turned to my academic accomplishments that night, my aunt, a college student at the time, left the table and returned with one of her college textbooks. She flipped to a random page in the center of the book and asked me if I could read it. I remember feeling nervous, but exhilarated, at the chance to show the adults in the room how well I could read, and I read the text without trouble, the slightest tremble evident in my voice. They praised me excitedly when I closed the book—and I've never quite forgotten that feeling. Accomplished. Proud. Talented. Able.

Approval and acceptance are among the most powerful feelings we can experience. When either of these is threatened, the natural response is to show the world that we are worthy of both. These emotions are so powerful that we easily become swept away in the act of proving ourselves without recognizing the truth of the matter: We have eternal approval and acceptance. We need not earn it. If I had been unable to read the passage in my aunt's college textbook, would my parents have loved me less? Not at all. Though I yearned to make them proud at that dinner table so many years ago, their approval and love never depended on my reading ability. It's the same with God. At His table, you are exceedingly loved, eternally accepted, and forever approved to sit with Him.

We have eternal approval and acceptance. We need not earn it.

What are you most scared of losing? Is it the approval you once felt or the rush of accomplishment when a goal was met? I don't believe God is asking you to lose all motivation to achieve goals. I do believe He's holding you by the shoulders and slightly shifting you to face a new direction that you'll walk together. The goals He will encourage you to set in the future will look a lot different from the ones you're used to, but God-set goals are the only ones you want to achieve anyway, right?

When we are secure in our position with our heavenly Father, competition and envy fade away. Suddenly, the mom in the checkout line next to you with the designer diaper bag and the screaming toddler is your sister in battle. Like you, she's just one naptime away from finding her serenity for the day.

None of us "have it all" at the same time. There is no perfect life. There is only Christ's perfect love, always present, always guiding us to turn to Him for a glimpse at the perfection our hearts long for. Don't be fooled by the feigned perfection that so many try to display. The mom with the perfectly matched outfits and silky-smooth hair doesn't have it all. She's one thrown sippy cup away from a breakdown too. We can't let ourselves get lost in wanting someone else's life. This is it. This is our allotted time to experience life with all of its tender beauty and aching sorrows. Let's not spend it comparing and despairing because we believe the lie that perfection is possible outside of Christ.

This is your path, your motherhood journey, and yours are the children God has entrusted to you. It doesn't all make sense right now. It really doesn't have to. For right now, serve God with all that you have, and be content to know that you are enough because He is enough. The rest will fall into place. You'll see.

⟶ Reflection Questions

1. When you reflect on the moment you decided to stay home, what are the prominent emotions you experience?

2. How has motherhood shifted your perspective on your purpose? Is it a welcomed or resented shift? Why?

⤳ Talk to Him About It

*Lord, show me how my desire to have
it all has blinded me to Your will for my
life. Guide me into the nearness with
You that I yearn to experience. Help me
release this fear that whispers that I'm not
enough as I am. I trust You, Lord. Amen.*

Making Room for Honesty

The Truths We Don't Expect

You will know the truth, and the truth will set you free.
John 8:32

The gray-haired woman in line ahead of me at the grocery store smiled knowingly as I gently bounced Bryce in the baby carrier I wore him in.

"Enjoy every moment; he'll be grown before you know it," she said. I returned her smile and replied that I knew he would grow quickly and I was truly trying to enjoy every moment.

I *was* enjoying motherhood, there in the checkout line, as I mindlessly rubbed his tiny sock-covered foot. I loved feeling his fuzzy head against my chest and the warmth of his tiny body next to mine. I traced each tiny toe and felt my stomach drop at the thought of him growing too large to be carried through the grocery store, cuddled close and in our own little world together.

I knew it was inevitable and that, though I tried, it was impossible to enjoy every moment. The mothers on magazines all smiled flawlessly back at me, their gazes showing no trace of stress. Even the woman on the nipple cream box smiled serenely at her baby. When I was in desperate need of nipple cream during the first days of nursing, I wasn't serene, and I wasn't smiling, that's for sure. *Was I doing this wrong? Was it possible to enjoy every moment?*

If you left your career willingly to be home with your children, you might feel a little uncomfortable admitting that you don't love it all the time. *I love it! It's so fun*, you probably tell others when they ask how you like it. Even on my worst days, I used to tell anyone who asked that I loved being home. *I'm enjoying it so much*, I'd lie through a smile. That's what a loving mother says about her new life of wiping mouths and the other end on a ceaseless loop, right? You don't want to admit that you are actually quite tired of feeling like diapers and dishes are the only things you do anymore. Or that you're exhausted and tired of giving because you have needs too.

Add an element of pride on top, like the cherry on a sundae you never ordered, and you've got a recipe for shame. Maybe you left your job with such excitement that you'd rather eat live crickets than admit to a former colleague that you feel deflated and as though maybe you made the wrong choice. Saying out loud that it's difficult—or downright miserable at times—can feel like you're being ungrateful, and that doesn't quite align with all of those Instagram pictures with the hashtag #blessed, does it? If I could reach through these words right now and hug you, I would.

Early on in my motherhood journey, after caring day in, day out for a high-needs infant with a dairy intolerance, I began to lose steam. The cracks in my smooth "I've got this" facade were beginning to show, and it wasn't pretty. Ed would arrive home to a wife smiling with a quivering chin, assuring him the day had been fine, but this "staying home thing" was different from what she expected. The dishes were done, the baby was cared for, and I was an emotional mess.

"I need to go back to work," I'd sob through tears, feeling guilt and shame for how ungrateful I must sound. He would recommend that I do just that and find a sitter to care for Bryce, so that I could return to the career I loved so much. I couldn't, though. The instant he suggested it, anger flared within me, and I'd brush off his suggestion as crazy. I loved my baby. I wanted to be home. *Why was I so conflicted?* I would argue, as much to him as to myself, that I was meant to stay home with our son. It must have been difficult (not to mention confusing) for Ed as I swung on the pendulum between blissful joy in being home with my baby and desperation for...something I couldn't put my finger on.

I felt stuck. I wasn't who I used to be, and whoever I was becoming was a stranger at best. I hated that I wasn't contributing financially to our home. Ed never made me feel an ounce of guilt over it, but internally I made up for what he didn't say. My own thoughts about my lack of worth and earning power played on repeat throughout the day. I refused to shop for myself and felt guilty making the smallest purchases even if I needed them. I knew that I needed to find a way to make peace with staying home and stop fighting the inevitable. I wasn't going back to work anytime soon, but I couldn't continue to feel so out of place in my own skin either. There had to be some secret that other mothers who loved being home knew, and I just had to figure it out.

It was time to get honest with myself. Each time I would take Bryce to the park to kill time and check off the "good mom" box for the day, I saw other mothers who seemed to thrive in their lives at home. They brought snacks and met up with other moms who, like them, seemed to be living their best lives. *What do they do all day—alone?* I would wonder to myself. *Are they really that happy to be home with their kids, making dinner and wiping Popsicle-smeared mouths?* It was then I knew there was a piece to my puzzle missing. They knew something—they *had* something—that I didn't.

Occasionally, I met someone who was only off for the summer or for maternity leave before she headed back to work, and I would field the usual questions about where I used to teach and why I resigned. Those moments stung more than I wanted to admit. It was always difficult to come face-to-face with the truth. Maybe you're at that point now, and you need to dig down to the root of why you feel so lost without a job or a business card with your name on it. Maybe it isn't the lack of a job, but the sacrifice of dreams you've put on hold that steals your passion for today. You were planning to advance, to make a name for yourself—and instead God is asking you to advance His name and place in your life. Let's just admit right now that it's hard. Let's acknowledge that all of it—the mothering, the letting go, the change—is so very hard. I know how it feels when ambitions have taken a backseat, and every day feels more draining than the last.

When we are in the midst of living our chaotic yet mundane lives—playing hide-and-seek and driving to the pediatrician's office for the third time in one month—it's easy to set our emotions aside. We power through, get it done, and soldier on. After all, bath time is coming up after dinner, but then there are still teeth to brush and medicines to give. By the time bedtime finally rolls around—after the countless drinks of water given, bedtime stories read, and prayers said—it's a miracle you can keep your eyes open. Ambition is nowhere to be found…and neither is whoever you used to be.

What is the missing puzzle piece? Why is this so hard? Part of the reason the transition to staying home was so difficult was that I wrongfully identified what was lacking. When I took a good, hard look, it wasn't the fact that I was no longer employed. Employment status had nothing to do with the spiritual ailment that affected every corner of my life. Have you done the same? Have you examined the truth about the uncomfortable feelings in your heart? As hard as this process is to make time for, we must be willing to come face-to-face with our deepest pain and truths.

For me, this process took an entire year as I struggled to make sense of my new normal. I decided that if I couldn't work outside of the home, I would work *from* home. It made logical sense to me at the time even though I knew in my gut it wasn't what the Lord had for me. I ignored the voice within and forged ahead. I applied for job after job—and received rejection after rejection.

The rejections stung with an intensity I hadn't anticipated. With every rejection, my determination to somehow find a loophole in God's will grew stronger. *I would just look at more job listings,* I decided. Chasing after a shiny new title felt a lot easier than admitting the honest truths in my heart. Getting a job became a new goal to accomplish—and reaching it would fill all the empty places in my self-worth. I would be needed again—for something other than diaper changes and unloading the dishwasher. I was going to prove that I could have it all.

It took an embarrassing number of job applications and subsequent rejections before my stubborn ego fully accepted the message God was sending in no uncertain terms. I was not going to win this battle. I allowed myself to cry the tears I needed to, even though they felt like weakness and defeat, and I eventually accepted that my plan to work from home was not meant to be.

I was angry with God for hurting my pride when, in reality, He was trying to show me that no job offer could provide the acceptance that He could. At the time, I understood, but I still sulked. His message was painful but clear: I was to stay home, focus on my child, and find out who I really was in Him without a job title of any kind. I felt the familiar sense that I was being disciplined after not listening to my Father, thinking I knew better. I knew He wasn't angry with me, but He would not allow me to escape sitting with myself and getting to the root of my unhappiness.

He would not allow me to escape sitting with myself and getting to the root of my unhappiness.

What's in a Title?

It's never about what you think it's about. My determination to find a way to work from home was not about financially contributing to our family. It was about where I found my own value. My struggle with confusing my identity with a title has shown itself a few times in my life. If I reflect back on a few key milestones in my life, I can see it clearly, though at the time I was completely blind to it.

There was the time in college when, about to graduate with my degree, I was offered two jobs. The salary for one of them was three times the other, but the lesser paying position had a better title. The word *manager* was attached to the end of it, and I loved the power that seemed to convey. The other job was for an executive assistant position. *Assistant* didn't have quite the same ring as *manager* did. It would feel really good to tell others I was a manager, straight out of college.

Looking back, I laugh at how conceited I must have sounded when I brought the "dilemma" to my college mentor. I'll never forget sitting in his office in the communications department. I told him of the two offers, and he congratulated me. When I told him I was confused about which job to take, he looked at me confoundedly.

"You take the higher paying job! What is there to think about?" he asked.

When I sheepishly admitted I didn't like the title of the more lucrative position, he laughed. "Titles don't put food on the table," he chuckled.

Hearing him put it that way was the reality check I needed to make my decision. He was right, and I accepted the executive assistant position.

You might think that I accepted the assistant position and put the entire job title issue behind me, but you would be wrong. I wish I could say that I did, but the loss of that sparkly title of "manager" still haunted me even as I sat at a desk earning a salary triple what I would have earned with that title.

Maybe you've been there too. Perhaps you've experienced the sting of a title that didn't feel like it fit what you were doing or *who you were*. Maybe it's the title of "Mom." It's one that we hold closest to our hearts—and one that we allow our emotions to dictate the truth about. Our emotions about this title swing from high highs to low lows, yet a permanence remains regardless of how we feel in the moment. Once the adrenaline has faded from birth and we settle into this new title—one that cannot be upgraded or changed—it becomes increasingly difficult to deny the truths about our own quest for validation.

When we are in the proper position of humility and submission to God, we openhandedly give Him the glory of any title He wishes to hold in our lives and hearts. *Creator. Counselor. Healer. The Great I AM.* These are only a few of the names used to describe our heavenly Father. These are the titles we should hold dear. Jesus is not interested in the titles you hold, but in the ones you allow Him to hold in your life.

> *Jesus is not interested in the titles you hold, but in the ones you allow Him to hold in your life.*

In the Gospel of Mark (8:29), Jesus asked His disciples first who men said He was and then who the disciples themselves thought He was. He asked, "But what about you? Who do you say I am?" (8:29). Jesus wanted to know who His closest friends thought Him to be.

Peter responded to Christ, "You are the Messiah" (verse 29). In Greek, *messiah* means "the anointed one, the chosen one." How about you? Is He the chosen One in your life? The One you hold high above all others? When we lose sight of Jesus' importance and His role in our lives, we easily allow things of this world to take His place. The loss of my teaching career became the light that exposed my wrongly held beliefs about who I really was and who He was in my life.

If I wasn't a teacher, who was I? Now that I was a mom, was everything I had worked for really going to just fade into the distance? The real question was *whose* I was. The very basic truth is...I was His.

> *The real question was whose I was.*

During premarital counseling, our therapist said something I will never forget. He placed his pen at the top of his yellow notepad, crossed his legs in the upholstered chair where he sat, and said gently, "Jen, we can change what we do without changing who we are."

At the time I related his advice to my impending marriage, but now I see that the truth of this statement permeates any season in life. Who we are is unchanged by what we do or what title we hold. Whether you're changing diapers or performing heart transplants, the bottom line is the same: You belong to God, and that is enough.

You belong to God, and that is enough.

How we really wrap our hearts and minds around that truth is as individual as we are. For some (ahem, yours truly), the idea that we are saved by grace—and that no amount of striving will save us any more than we already are—is difficult to comprehend. We've become so used to climbing ladders and kicking at glass ceilings that grace no longer feels real. The push to strive for more and to be more has been the way of life that has led to success—and now it's come to a screeching halt. If you're not pushing your way ahead of the competition anymore, then what are you to do?

Allowing yourself the time to sit in silence and consider the ways you're fighting God—consciously or unconsciously—about His plan for you is a good starting point. What are the questions you are afraid to ask Him? Are your fears connected more to the present or to what will happen in the future? It will probably feel uncomfortable—awkward even—to sit in stillness before God. Keep sitting, staying with Him. The sitting I'm talking about does not require that you physically sit. It's a posture of your heart.

When we sit before God in surrender, looking for answers and guidance, we humbly open ourselves to His will for our lives. His answers probably won't come immediately, but He honors persistence. We can and should bring our questions before Him, knowing

He is faithful to answer and our confidence comes through Christ. He will always meet you where you are.

I can remember a time when God spoke so clearly it took my breath away. One summer afternoon I stood in the garage next to my car and began to feel sweat prickling my back. I had been standing there for a good ten minutes, begging Bryce to sit in his car seat so I could take him to the park. Standing up in his car seat, he literally dug his heels into the padded cover and shook his head no. "GWATH!" he shrieked over and over. He wanted to play in the backyard where the *grass* was.

His forehead was beaded with sweat, and his round cheeks were flushing a brighter shade of pink than usual. "Mommy wants to take you to the park!" I pleaded. "The park—with the swings and the trees! It has a big slide! Don't you want to go to the park?"

His response was more shrieking, sweating, and fist clenching. He wasn't hearing a word I said. The park I wanted to take him to was beautiful. Filled with mature trees and a play structure that I knew he would love—if only he would allow me to show him.

I was working hard to make the case that the park was much better than our backyard. I needed to get us both out of the house and out of the endless cycle of worry about submitting my resignation. It felt so final. So unknown. The future felt like one big question mark. I needed to go to the park. I needed a change of scenery. I needed to escape the voice in my head that told me I could not expect a positive outcome if I ignored the voice of God asking me to let my career go. Surely God knew how much my work meant to me—He had led me to get my teaching credential to begin with! Maybe I just needed more time to convince Him to reconsider.

Bryce did not want to hear all of the benefits of the park. He could only focus on how much he did not want to go. He loved our backyard, and it was good enough for him. He wanted what he had seen, what he knew. He was not willing to trust that I knew he would enjoy the park more. My legs began to ache as I stood next to the open car door, pleading harder for him to just sit down so we could go. That's when I heard Him.

God whispered to my heart that, in my own way, I was behaving no differently than my toddler. God told me there was an unknown place of beauty He wanted to take me to, but I did not trust Him enough to follow. I wanted to stay where I was, with what I had known. The truth was, I had never known the reality of working and having a child. I only knew what it was to enjoy my career separate from motherhood.

My heart was waging an epic war with my mind that said I could be everything I ever wanted to be and have all the things I wanted to have...all at the same time. God wasn't calling me to that, however, and I was throwing a fit. If ever there were a picture that summed up my internal behavior, it was the sweaty little boy, with his clenched fists, protesting right in front of me. The truth hurt, but in so many ways it felt a lot like relief, to hear God speak in no uncertain terms. He spoke through a simple interaction with my son, but His message was undeniable, and He couldn't have been clearer. For the first time, I understood. Standing firm in my stubbornness seemed safer than following God and His plan for my life, but it was not the right choice.

What to Do When Fear Takes Over

Maybe you, too, have struggled with God's idea for the path you are to take. Perhaps you're not behaving like a red-faced toddler in a fit of stubbornness, but you're fighting the life set before you in ways you haven't fully recognized. The future feels unknown, and what you once planned has been washed away by the tidal wave of motherhood. So much of what we fear is due to the uncertainty of the future. Even those with the most determined of plans cannot foretell the future. Only God knows what the next day, hour, or even minute will hold. For those of us who love to be in control, this is a tough pill to swallow. Sometimes, as hard as we try, we hold on to our fears and don't release them to God as He asks.

Most of the time we only release our fears when we are faced with them head-on. We like evidence-based faith, don't we? Blind faith feels much too risky. Irresponsible even. The truth is, our fears present us with an opportunity to exercise our faith in new and uncomfortable ways.

We can take our struggle and anxiety about the unknown straight to God. He's the only One truly equipped to take it from us. The enemy will try to convince us repeatedly that we need to see our fear, touch it, experience it in order to believe God is capable of releasing us from the anxiety it creates, but we have to remember that the enemy has always been—and forever will be—a liar. Not only does Jesus know your struggle, but He has given you the faith you require to overcome it.

Maybe you wonder whether you'll ever re-enter the work world again. You worry you'll be sorely unprepared, having taken such a lengthy break from it all. Your coworkers have continued their education and professional growth—and you have not. While they accepted awards and earned promotions, you've learned how to navigate the store without passing the toy aisle, which cartoons have high-pitched voices you refuse to allow in your home, and how many M&Ms it takes to bribe your toddler to poop. Not only have you stepped away from the path you once planned for yourself, but you've completely disappeared from the map altogether. You're fearful, anxious, and unsure.

God wants to hear about it. We were never meant to keep our

struggles to ourselves even if our struggles are related to following Him. Letting go of receiving recognition from others is a process. Acknowledging that we depend on it in a spiritually unhealthy way is the first step to healing. Giving up a daily routine with scheduled breaks is no small thing—and you likely realized this in your first months home. After the new wears off and the feeling of an endless vacation begins to lose its shine, reality sets in. All of a sudden your entire day revolves around nap times, lunchtimes, and playtimes—a far cry from what you used to know. It's okay to admit that you miss your career. This is an uncomfortable but necessary step in accepting your calling to be home. You're not a bad mother or ungrateful if you feel torn between the life you had and the very different one you live now.

Emotions coexist. Your left hand may hold pain while your right holds contentment or joy. The very fact that you are reading this book and want to be the best possible version of yourself proves your love and dedication to your children. Go ahead and tell God about what you miss— even the things you deem silly or nonsensical. Perhaps you miss the long drive to work, alone with your thoughts and the radio. Maybe it was shopping guilt-free for work clothes. Whatever it might be, if it matters to you, it matters to God.

One business trip I took during my time at the nonprofit is slightly more memorable than the many I took during my marketing career. It's taken me a lot of thought and reflection to understand why. On this particular trip I flew to a conference in Washington, D.C., with a female coworker, each of us engaged to be married at the time. We spent the three-day trip watching our carb intake, working out in the hotel gym, and touring the monuments and museums.

On our last day there, during a visit to the National Zoo, the beautiful spring weather shifted within moments to an incredible storm with raging winds and rain. At the gift shop, we purchased animal print umbrellas—that were promptly turned inside out by the whipping wind outside. Soaked from head to toe, she and I couldn't help but laugh at our pitiful appearances. We looked as though we had just emerged from a swimming pool, fully clothed in business casual. We tried for several minutes to hail a cab in the downpour, and we watched helplessly as one after another drove past without slowing. Finally, one merciful cabdriver picked us up and delivered us back to the hotel where we changed our clothes and got ready to meet for dinner. The day was exhausting but fun, and even when we returned home from the trip, we talked about it often.

When I reflect back on this trip, it's not the monuments or the travel that make me reminisce about my career. It's the feeling of being self-sufficient and the carefree joy that I remember most fondly. The ability to plan my time and activities with no one else to worry about is something that I miss. There were no strollers to worry about when climbing aboard a tour bus and no nap schedule to manage my day around. I hope it goes without saying that I love spending time with my family, as I'm certain you do, but it was lovely to be able to choose dining options based upon my food preferences, not the kids' menu.

Perhaps for you it's not the ability to travel alone or choose restaurants without nuggets and fries on the menu. Maybe you miss the simple act of making a cup of coffee in the quiet of a break room even though you have coffee every morning at home. Maybe it's the small talk you engaged in each Monday morning, catching up with colleagues about the past weekend. These small things are actually some of the big things. Tell God all that you miss about your life before kids even if it feels silly. You might surprise yourself with your own prayers.

Reflection Questions

1. When conflicting emotions about motherhood arise, is your first instinct to accept and move through them, or to shame yourself for having them? Explain.

2. Has God ever tried to send you a message that you were intent on ignoring? What was it—and why did you try to ignore it?

3. How has fear of the unknown impacted you in motherhood? Be specific.

4. What titles do you cling to for your sense of worth?

Talk to Him About It

Father, I try so hard to get it all right. I want to be the mom You had in mind when You blessed me with a child. Forgive me for placing my worth in any title other than Daughter of God. Help me to hear Your voice and discern Your will for my life in this season. Father, I trust You.

This Was Not in the Job Description

Dealing with Your Ego Gracefully

Humble yourselves before the Lord, and he will lift you up.
James 4:10

Giggling uncontrollably, Bryce had just thrown yet another greasy fistful of hot dog pieces onto the floor. They rested next to macaroni and cheese that had begun to harden and stick to the tile grout. On my hands and knees, picking up the thrown food, I was fighting the tears that burned my eyes and formed a lump in my throat. *I'm so sick of this.* I thought. *I have a college degree! What was it for? This? THIS?* I directed my inward screaming to no one in particular because I wasn't brave enough to direct it toward God. He knew, as He always does, that it was meant for Him. Right then I heard Him whisper, clear and to the point, *This is serving. This is loving Me.* I wish I could say that His kind response changed my attitude immediately, and I began to whistle while I worked. It did not.

Maybe you've been there too. Cleaning a kitchen floor, wiping a toilet seat, vacuuming crumbs out of the couch one more time, and you catch yourself thinking, *I'm worth more than this. All of that work—all of those dreams—led me* here? These questions can steal your joy.

They come from an ugly place within—one we don't want to readily admit exists. We would rather brush over these inconvenient places within that we like to think hold Christ-like humility and meekness. When these blemishes are not dealt with properly, rest assured they'll rear their heads at the most inopportune and embarrassing moments. A correction of your child's behavior that you meant to be gentle will land sharply and loudly. Simple mistakes will receive no grace, especially those you make yourself. Bitterness will set up shop with those who know you best (and love you most) coming to expect harsh, sarcastic responses.

I paint an ugly picture, but it's a canvas many of us have grown accustomed to living on. This is not who you wanted to be when you became a stay-at-home mom, I know. The truth is, in order for us to reach God's best, He sometimes allows us to first come face-to-face with the worst.

Not only is our family's peace hanging in the balance, but so is the message we send to our children. Kids are incredibly perceptive, and when our children see us frustrated and unsatisfied with what life has dealt us, we communicate that what we have is not enough to bring contentment—and, in essence, that they themselves aren't enough. None of us want that to be the message our children receive. I want my boys to feel loved and wanted beyond measure. When I was teaching, the students of a colleague told her that they never wanted to have children of their own. When my friend told me this, I was confused: Why would third-graders already have such firm beliefs about their future as parents? "Because their parents don't make them feel wanted. These parents are struggling, and they most likely tell these kids regularly how easy life was before they were born," she replied. The idea that these children felt unwanted, felt like a burden in their own homes, struck me.

It stayed with me as I began creating my own family. No matter how difficult life becomes, I don't want my children to ever feel unwanted. I want our home to be a place of love, acceptance, and warm memories. Our personal circumstances and external behavior, for better or for worse, set the tone of our homes. It's a sacred responsibility that rests upon our shoulders to be the ones who establish the temperature in the household. In order to do this in the way God would choose, we first have to be aware—and stay aware—of our impact in our own homes.

This awareness requires a constant humility and a willingness to adjust—for the greater good of our family—our attitudes and behavior as necessary. That's not to say it will be easy or convenient; in fact, the opposite is true. We are given repeated opportunities in motherhood to hone this particular skill, and even when we think we've grown quite adept at it, we'll be proven otherwise.

A few years ago, I took a rare break to get a pedicure at a local salon—something I try to do at least once a summer. When I arrived home with freshly painted toes, the boys wanted to go on a walk around the neighborhood. Ed and I packed the boys into the double stroller and off we went, leisurely enjoying the mild evening. We were almost home when Bryce decided he wanted to walk instead of ride in the stroller, and he accidentally put his sneakered foot onto my toes to disembark. Startled and in midstride, I stubbed my toe badly on the stroller wheel. As you can guess, my big toe (the most important toe, as any woman knows) suffered the brunt of the sudden stop, and my freshly painted toenail was now broken and chipped.

I instantly became angry and fought back tears the rest of the way home. Ed couldn't understand why I was so upset at the innocent mistake. The truth was, I wasn't really upset about the destroyed pedicure—the accident just felt like *one more thing*. Have you ever been in that situation, when the one time you try to do something *for yourself for a change,* turns out to be more trouble than it's worth? When on top of everything else you're having feelings about, something else is suddenly piled on—and it's a straw that is perilously close to breaking the camel's back?

That's what my broken toenail represented. One more way that I was getting forgotten. One more way I was misunderstood. One more reason to throw a pity party for myself, for the broken-toenailed, overworked, and underappreciated mother of two I had become. I giggle at it now, but at the time, in my state of exhaustion and exasperation, it was anything but funny.

Worship While You Work

Perception is key.

If we fail to take responsibility for our own attitude and well-being, we will forever feel as though we are deserving of endless pity from our family. Serving our family is a holy responsibility with eternal ramifications. God has given us these souls to care for during our time on Earth. We can view this as a privilege instead of a burden (while still managing healthy boundaries for self-care) and grow into the wife and mother God intended us to be. Imagine, for a moment, that when Jesus washed His disciples' feet, He sighed heavily and asked each of them, "Do you know who I am? I shouldn't be doing this." It's an uncomfortable image, right? Jesus is kind, meek, lowly in heart, and came to serve. He gave the example of serving His disciples so that we, too, would serve one another.

This doesn't mean that if you just love Jesus enough, you'll one day love cleaning toilets. What it does mean is that the daily pouring out of ourselves into our children can be seen as an act of love for God. Our work is not our worth, but our work can be our worship.

The unreached goals of your past may whisper in your ear that they will sit unaccomplished forever—and it's tempting to believe that voice.

Our work is not our worth,
but our work can be our worship.

Maybe you received a degree or certification and never had the chance to put it to use before babies were on the horizon. Perhaps, like me, you had a career—or a few—and didn't realize the sense of importance that grew out of your titles and accomplishments. In either scenario, the issue is about your heart more than it is your circumstances.

Our egos assert their importance in a variety of ways, and oftentimes they've been steadily doing so for years without our noticing. Have you ever struggled when you did not receive proper credit for an achievement? Maybe at work, a coworker stole your thunder in front of a supervisor. For those of us who tie our self-worth to achievement, this is always frustrating—if not downright infuriating.

Something always seems to wait in the wings, ready to tarnish our joy and take away the shine. I've been there. The last time this happened, I replayed the scene repeatedly in my mind (not exactly the best strategy for finding a resolution). My anger was palpable, and I started telling God exactly what I thought, that I deserved the credit. He listened for a while before I heard His voice speak to my heart that I didn't need to be angry.

The person who took the credit from me was wrong, but so was I. God alone was the One who gave me the gifts and skills to accomplish anything I do. He watched from the sidelines as I fought in my head needless battles about who deserved what acknowledgment when, really, I needed to turn my eyes upward and give credit where credit was due.

We can do nothing of value apart from God. Until we get that straight, not only in our minds but also in the core of our beings, we will continue to run in circles fighting with ourselves. When the voices in our heads tell us we have every right to demand justice and credit, we actually have yet another opportunity to humble ourselves before Christ.

When the voices in our heads tell us we have every right to demand justice and credit, we actually have yet another opportunity to humble ourselves before Christ.

It is one thing to feel a sense of pride in your accomplishments, knowing you followed God's lead and brought joy to the Father's heart. It's entirely different to boast of your own power and ability without acknowledging the One who gave you the ability to begin with, opened the doors you walked through, and provided you with the strength to finish the work.

John the Baptist spent his entire life preparing others for the coming Savior and then spreading the news once Jesus made Himself known as God in the flesh. John's entire life was one of service that God had ordained before his birth. In the book of Luke, we learn that John physically leaped in Elizabeth's womb simply from being in the presence of unborn Jesus (Luke 1:41). John's life had an incredible purpose, but it was not one that was comprised of his own plans and dreams. In contrast, John's life was a vessel for God's plan alone. When others wondered if John himself was the Messiah, he was quick to deny the claim and point them to the Savior whose sandals he was not fit to untie (Luke 3:16). John's was a life of humility and service that is forever recorded in the very Word of God.

The humility of John exemplifies the beauty of serving Christ with no personal gain in mind. Even when our hearts are in the right place, life at home can feel tedious and repetitive. My boys have a playroom filled with toys, many of which they don't play with. When Ed and I dedicated a room specifically for toys, we had grand visions of our boys playing in the room for hours on end, overjoyed to have a room designated for their favorite possessions.

The reality is, they hardly ever play in the playroom. Most days a trail of Legos, action figures, and superhero capes snakes its way out the door and into the living room. For much of the day, I try to ignore it, stepping over toys and focusing on the work around the house that feels more permanent. I know that if I pick their toys up, they'll only make their way back out a few minutes later. Housework feels pointless: The dishes seem to multiply in the sink as soon as the table is cleared, and the laundry is never completely done unless you do laundry naked—which is tempting, just to be able to say it is *all* washed.

If what we produce or work for isn't permanent, is it still worth doing? It might not feel like it is, but even temporary work has permanent results. All the little things you do over and over every day are seen by God. If you could watch your life like a movie on fast-forward, you would see that the dishes, laundry, books, snuggles, tantrums (by you or the children), and even the socks you pull out of the corners of the couch on a much-too-regular basis add up to a life of authenticity and love.

Deciding Who Kills the Spiders

Let's talk for a moment about housework. I mentioned in chapter 2 that for a short period of time, I avoided the difficulty of staying home by doing housework. It became a sort of obsession to hide the emotions that I knew were just waiting to spill out into the open, betraying the external facade of an incredibly happy (and #blessed!) stay-at-home mom. When you first begin this transition into stay-at-home mothering, the entire family transitions with you. This means that previous expectations of who does what have now been turned on their head—and if this change is not acknowledged, it is a recipe for disaster and a barrier to peace in your home.

When I was working, and we only had ourselves to worry about, Ed and I lived the lives that I imagine most childless couples do. We both worked hard, came home exhausted, and whoever felt charitable that day loaded the dishwasher or did a load of laundry. Ed is incredibly self-sufficient, and neither of us depended on the other for much around the house. Ed took care of all outdoor chores like mowing the lawn and weeding. He was elected CSK (chief spider killer) from the start. I rarely cooked because I didn't feel confident about my cooking skills, and it felt pointless to make anything for just the two of us.

I had many failed meal attempts confirm my suspicions that I was not meant to be a chef. As a result, most evenings I ate cereal for dinner before Ed arrived home late. When he got home, he threw together whatever he could manage, and though I felt a twinge of guilt watching him raid our refrigerator after a long day at work, it wasn't enough for me to put all the hours I spent watching DVR'd Rachael Ray to use. I resented that no one premeasured my ingredients in little glass jars ahead of time, and I added that to the list of reasons why cooking was too much work in real life.

Ed and I spent time together on weeknights watching television and reading until it was time for bed, only to begin the cycle again the next day. Once a newborn was in the picture, life was—as expected—thrown upside down for a time. Once we had a routine in place (feed the baby, change the baby, rock the baby, repeat), my season of striving to earn the Best Homemaker Ever medal gave way to a season of being unmotivated to match the socks, much less make dinner. Life was no longer recognizable, and I knew that our habits at home needed a makeover. If life is forever changed by having a child, then that included the way Ed and I functioned within our home as well. The guilt I felt watching my husband do his own laundry for work was palpable.

I was home all day, and yet I hid behind the excuse that caring for my baby was all consuming. There's no denying that caring for an infant is time-consuming, but even as a new parent who rarely set her baby down, I knew I had time to throw in a load of clothes to be washed or put food in the slow cooker for dinner.

Ed never said a word to me about it—he knew I was struggling to figure out what was happening and who I was. It wasn't until one night when he gently asked if I would be willing to throw a load of his clothes in the washing machine to help him prepare for the following week, or maybe make a meal here and there for dinner, that the full wave of guilt finally washed over me. Shame and embarrassment overtook me, and I knew it was time I either owned this life of being a "domestic engineer" or gave it up entirely. After offering weak defenses for why I hadn't done so earlier, I agreed to help him however I could.

I had immediately felt defensive, but it came from a place of shame and embarrassment, not righteous anger. Looking back, I can't quite put my finger on what kept me from seeing what my husband needed and deserved from me as a partner, except that I was depressed and feeling lost. I had swung on the pendulum from striving to be the best stay-at-home mom possible to being one who didn't want to do housework out of fear it would define who she was. It was as if an unspoken belief had taken root somewhere in my mind that if I took care of the household and the husband I married, I was admitting defeat.

Maybe it was all of the messages I had inadvertently received while growing up in the eighties. The encouragement that I could do anything and be anything I wanted to be had become my stumbling block to finding contentment in the simple and humble tasks of living. I *could* do anything I wanted, but it felt wrong to want only to raise my child and be home. The shockwaves of this new life and what it entailed had traveled through both Ed and me, and we were scrambling to discover the best way to support one another. At the time, I didn't recognize the importance of my role and my true acceptance of my new place in our family.

This is a sticky area for couples, isn't it? No one wants to revert to outdated expectations and stereotypes of what men or women are responsible for in a household. Ed and I eventually muddled through some tense moments while we ironed out (see what I did there?) our intrinsic beliefs about what we deserved from one another, but I believe there's a better way—and I wish I would have found it sooner. You know, before all the petty arguments over who was responsible for cleaning out the refrigerator and dusting the blinds with the correct vacuum attachment began.

Before any kind of decisions can be made about who does what, there needs to be an acknowledgment that things are different now. You are in the home, and he's at work. For him, life might very much look the same during the day except for your text messages reminding him that he's later than he said he would be and that it's been a long day for you. For you, life looks nothing like it used to.

When we married our husbands, we promised to be a partner, and with that promise comes responsibilities. I encourage you to think about what you know of your husband and what he needs from you. (I know, at this point you might be thinking that you can't possibly give—and shouldn't have to give—any more than you already do. But keep reading. He's not off the hook either.)

Maybe he never has time to throw his lunch together before work and ends up eating fast food daily. Your making his lunch before bed every night might be a huge stress relief for him that takes very little effort for you.

If you haven't discussed housework already in your relationship, now is the time to talk about it: Which household tasks really matter to him because they make the difference between a house that feels chaotic and one that feels peaceful? What chore do you absolutely hate and wish you never had to do again? Talk about it. The answers for everyone will be different, but discussing this delicate topic can save you from unnecessary strain in your marriage.

Laying the groundwork for task division is so important because housework usually has more emotion tied to it than it should. Not to mention, if you're working hard to make sure his shirts are ironed each week, but all he really wants is a freshly vacuumed living room when he gets home, you're wasting time as a partner to your husband in a way that doesn't really make him feel loved the way he prefers. This goes both ways, of course.

If he's putting the kids to bed each night, but what you really need is help with bath time instead, he could be using his remaining energy for the day in a much more useful way. Also, it must be said, the time to discuss what you need is *not* when you're in the middle of needing it. I know it's tempting to yell down from the bathroom during bath time, when you're certain he's reading the news on his phone while on the toilet downstairs, *Some help up here would be nice!* It isn't exactly motivating to your partner.

After you've spent time learning what he feels are the keys to a peaceful home and sharing your own thoughts, start the negotiations. What will he do and what will you do as you both work to keep your home running well? Know that the bulk of the housework will most likely fall to you—not because you're a put-upon housewife from the fifties, but because you're the one who is home the majority of the time. If he were home and it was you who worked outside of the house, you would expect that he would do the same to help life run smoothly. Let's also not forget that there must be a clear understanding between you both of the reality of keeping a home livable while also living in it *with children*.

Once upon a time I believed that it would be easy to keep our home constantly looking showcase-ready...before two little people came into our lives that proved me to be the wrongest person who ever lived. It's hard work—and sometimes I wonder if Ed understands how difficult it truly is to keep all four million toys in the playroom and the kitchen counters clear. He does, I know. When I've left the boys with him to run errands, I often return to find him wondering aloud how I ever get anything done during the week. It's often just the validation I need to continue being the Wonder Woman of my own home.

I'm always amazed at how quickly my home goes from clean to cluttered when my kids are just simply living their lives in the house. I've heard from many friends working outside the home that their homes stay cleaner longer simply because they aren't there most of the time. Ours is a blessed, albeit frustrating, problem to have.

As you discuss what division of labor will work best in your own home, don't be afraid to let the typical gender-based expectations go. If you would rather take out the trash or mow the lawn than do the grocery shopping, then why not switch it up? I would be remiss in talking about the subject of delineating housework without also mentioning the most important ingredient: a relationship built on partnership instead of pride.

A relationship must be built on partnership instead of pride.

If the idea of speaking to your husband about sharing the household duties adds more angst to your life, then I encourage you to pray about how you can strengthen your marriage first before you broach a subject that you know will only be divisive. A good marital relationship is not one that keeps a constant tally of who took the trash out last, but one that is free-flowing with grace and forgiveness.

There has to be a basic understanding that there will be days when the agreements you made won't be upheld. When you've had a busy day out, handling doctors' appointments and heading to the store for drain cleaner (because postpartum hair loss is no joke), you probably won't have time to also pick up the toys strewn throughout the house and make dinner—it's one or the other. I pray I'm preaching to the choir here and your relationship is one that values partnership and reciprocity above pride.

Making your home a place where peace reigns matters. I know it's difficult to separate the things that must be done from how they make us feel as we do them, but once you master the art of finding the true meaning behind serving your family with this kind of work, it becomes easier to do it with a willing heart. In so many ways, the mother in any home is the hub that makes the entire family wheel turn. When we accept this truth and the great responsibility it carries, we can humbly give thanks to God for entrusting us with the holy work that takes place at home. The preparation we provide our families makes all the difference in how they experience life.

Making Straight Paths

Earlier I mentioned the one man in the Bible who spent all his days preparing: John the Baptist spent his life making straight the path for the Lord. He spent his days endlessly pointing others to Jesus; it was his sole purpose in life. In our own homes, we can prepare a path for Jesus to walk into the hearts of our children. We can make the path straight early on so that knowing Jesus and His love is a natural step for our kids. The hard question we must ask is this: Where are we pointing? Is it straight to ourselves or to Jesus? There's a humility required if we are to point to Jesus and not to ourselves. It requires repeated apologies for when we get it wrong—and you will get it wrong. That's part of being human.

I apologize to my children frequently—for raising my voice, overreacting, not playing with them the moment they ask. The list goes on and on. Some people might argue that doing so gives children too much power or control in the home. I don't subscribe to that belief in the least. I want my boys to learn empathy and to know that I'm a work in progress. I'm far from perfect, and I want them to know that I'm aware of this fact. The more flaws I own up to, the more they can plainly see Jesus' forgiveness in my life and—I pray—receive it one day in theirs too. I hope, along the way, they will also learn to forgive themselves for their own mistakes.

The more flaws I own up to, the more they can plainly see Jesus' forgiveness in my life.

A few weeks ago, while driving Bryce to a meeting at school, I apologized to my boys for overreacting earlier in the day. It had been one of those mornings when I was louder than I ever need to be when I'm making a point, and the guilt was sitting heavy on my shoulders like an unwanted blanket. His response to my apology was one that beautifully showed the depth of his love for me, and I won't soon forget it. "I'll never stop forgiving you, Mom. I'll forgive you over and over," he said. I responded that I would do the same. I will always forgive him when he makes mistakes.

My earnest offering of unconditional forgiveness came easily to me. The depth of my love for my children is endless, and I desperately want them to know that it is unchanging and eternal. I realized during this short conversation with my six-year-old that it was also a teaching opportunity.

"You know, buddy, that's what Jesus does," I added. "He forgives us over and over again."

Bryce smiled and nodded from the backseat of the car. Some might argue that an offer of endless forgiveness is an invitation to abuse it—but I don't agree with that. I believe that the feeling of security that such a promise creates will only lead to a greater level of respect and love. The unconditional love of Christ never fails to soften my heart and straighten my own steps.

These unexpected and seemingly small moments are opportunities in our lives to become humble and allow Jesus to take center stage. If I hadn't apologized to my kids in that moment, this conversation never would have happened. Humility is the open door in our hearts that Jesus walks through.

Whatever you did before—and no matter how useful to God's kingdom, no matter how prestigious your title, no matter how much fulfillment you received from the accolades—God is calling you to walk a different path in this moment. He knows how much your previous work meant to you. He was there. He knows that you miss your work-friends and that this season of life feels lonely and monotonous. He knows. When the laundry is piled high, the children are screaming, and you feel like running away, He is there in the chaos, a witness to the work no one else sees. You have been called to this moment, and God knows you can handle it...with Him.

On your own, the weighty responsibility of raising children in this world is much too heavy to bear. When we partner with the One who assigned us this holy title of "Mom," we can walk with confidence into all He has planned for us and our babies. He's got this, rest assured.

Our circumstances do not have to dictate the state of our heart. The apostle Paul praised God from within his prison walls. He refused to let his circumstances control his spirit. His calling was too big to be hampered by a change in scenery. Yours is too. Something beautiful is happening within the walls of home. A family is being built. Love is being cultivated. Bodies are being nourished. This calling to raise children and praise God while doing so is nothing short of extraordinary. You may have done incredibly important and meaningful work before, but may I tell you something? You'll never be more important than who you are to God—and your family.

Though the work of motherhood sounds simple, it is anything but easy. No one knows your children as you do. The very hearts God knit together for your family beat for the care only you can provide. A mother's heart knows how to reach her child in a way that no one else can. Every day can be a struggle inside the four walls of home, but home can be a place of beauty as well. This everyday grind that threatens to pull you down and wring you dry of inspiration is not bigger than the purpose that God has put on your life with the children in your care.

The hidden truth in the middle of the daily life spent within the walls of home is that chances are, whatever you used to do for a living is now being used on a daily basis, perhaps without your even being aware. Think for a moment about how many times a day you're called to multitask, something I do on an hourly basis without paying much attention. As a teacher and marketer, I constantly found myself handling more than one critical situation at a time—and I found that most of the time I enjoyed the feeling of being able to do so. These days I'm preparing dinner while reviewing addition facts with my oldest and playing fetch with the dog. Multitasking at its finest—and it can take several forms in your life.

If you were a skilled negotiator in your previous position, I can guarantee you that if you have children aged three and older, you'll be involved in some intense negotiations that rival anything you've experienced. My toddler once negotiated himself a $20 toy at Target after I firmly denied I would purchase anything over $5. Toddler negotiation skills are not to be underestimated.

Our decision to homeschool our children was assisted by the fact that I was, in fact, a teacher and knew I could navigate my way through the elementary years with the boys. It's been the most rewarding teaching experience of my life, and I'm so grateful we have had the opportunity. This is, of course, an obvious way my previous career has come to be used in our current lives, and there are hundreds of other ways my job skills play out every day in our home. It's no different for you. If you ever had a needy, demanding, and impatient boss, you are well prepared for this new role of stay-at-home mothering.

While it's tempting to buy into the belief that what you're doing is "just" mothering and housekeeping, don't do it. Your past has prepared you for this role, and you are uniquely equipped for it. Those very skills you honed with pride are the same ones you'll pull out of your back pocket when you need them most. All of those late hours tirelessly working at the office translate into an endurance you'll need when a little one is sick and sleep is nowhere to be found. The way you learned to delicately deliver bad news to hopeful ears in a staff meeting translates into an uncanny ability to educate your third-grader that a smartphone will not be under the tree for many more Christmases. Your ability to keep the company budget in the black will help you do the same for your family finances. God wastes nothing when we are using our skill set and our hearts to follow and honor His will.

> *God wastes nothing when we are using our skill set and our hearts to follow and honor His will.*

God will meet you where you need Him most. He will go to any lengths to communicate His love to you—Jesus is proof of that. God met me on my kitchen floor, scrubbing macaroni and cheese out of tile grout and swallowing the tears that threatened to fall. In that moment, I was on my knees, and if my heart had been humble, I could have viewed it as an opportunity to worship God by serving my family. At the time, however, my heart was not in a position of worship. I was too stubborn and prideful, attending my own pity party decorated with streamers of self-importance.

Only now do I see that my acts of service for my children can be offered up as worship to God. We can serve the ones placed in our care with the love we ourselves have been lavished with by Jesus. The question is "Are you taking the time to tap into the endless well of His love, to acknowledge all of the ways He has been good and kind in your life?" We can't give what we aren't consciously aware that we have.

My acts of service for my children can be offered up as worship to God.

Once we humble ourselves and accept this incredible responsibility of mothering with servant hearts, we can worship God with our work. We will always be a reflection of Christ when we find ourselves humbly serving others. Motherhood is filled with moments when our egos will threaten to bare their teeth once more, hungry to show our existence and importance in the world. That's the path to popularity here, to carry our accomplishments high on our shoulders for the world and our social media followers to see. But God sees the work of your day that no one else sees. He sees the baths drawn, the floors swept, the tears wiped, and the foreheads kissed.

My boys love to pick me dandelions in our backyard. There's not much that melts my heart more than seeing a pudgy fist clenched around a wilted weed hidden behind a toddler's back. I place each flower, no matter how squished by little hands, into my Bible. It's where I keep my most treasured offerings. My youngest son, Bradley, will ask, "Are you proud of me, Mama? It's a big one!" I reassure him that I'm always proud of him and will be forever. And it's true. Their gifts of love mean so much to this mama's heart, but it has nothing to do with my love or pride. What they do for me does not affect my love for them. This is true of God's love for you as well.

Both of my boys are tenderhearted and will often begin enthusiastically telling me about one of their interests. I listen intently, excited to hear what they'll say next. Sometimes Bryce will preface his stories with "I know you're not into this, Mom, but..." and I stop him right there. "If it matters to you, it matters to me," I respond while looking into his eyes. I want my children to know that their interests and goals are important to me, and I want to see them achieve whatever they feel God is calling them to do. As a mom, that's my heart for them— and it's God's heart for them and for us.

Finally, you probably feel the same about your children that I feel about mine: Their joy is your joy, and the whispers of their heart matter to yours. It's no different with God. He knows what you desire, what you need, what you feel is missing. If it matters to you, it matters to Him. He is a God of details who cares about your life. Don't worry about identifying just yet that thing your soul is whispering. You'll get there. For now, rest in the knowledge that God knows what it is, and in His time, you will too.

Your heavenly Father is proud of you. He loves your gifts of service, and He sees them—but He does not require them. What you do for Him is not what you are worth to Him. He wants your heart. He sees your eagerness to please Him even if you feel as though all you have to offer are weeds.

Let's set our hearts on something more than the applause of man. Let's focus more on making certain that God has our whole heart, weeds and all, in complete surrender to Him. His goals are our goals. When we never want to be anywhere but in His will, we never get lost.

Reflection Questions

1. What mundane chores cause your ego to make an appearance?

2. How does housework make you feel emotionally?

3. What emotions arise as you consider being vulnerable enough to apologize to your children?

4. How can you offer up as worship your acts of service in the home and the lives of your children? Be specific.

Talk to Him About It

Lord, I confess that my ego often tries to take center stage, and I let it. Help me to stay vigilant and guard my heart and tongue against the temptation to believe that I'm more important than the chores and mundane activities of daily life. Use the things of my daily life to honor You, Father. Use me, in my home, to bring You glory. Lord, I trust You. Amen.

Netflix and Pajamas

Handling the Assumptions and Judgments of Others

He didn't mind how he looked to other people,
because the nursery magic had made him Real, and
when you are Real shabbiness doesn't matter.
Margery Williams, *The Velveteen Rabbit*[1]

Her tone of voice stung as she barely concealed her envy. "You're so lucky. We could never afford for me to stay home." Silenced and not knowing how to respond, I found a way to excuse myself from the conversation. She was a coworker and friend, and though I knew my decision to leave teaching for an extended amount of time was surprising, her comments made me doubt my choice.

It wasn't just this one person. Over and over, friends and coworkers told me how lucky I was to be able to resign and stay home. I knew they meant no real harm with their words, but the lack of certainty I already felt about my decision only grew each time I heard them. I had felt God speak clearly, yet voices from the outside threatened repeatedly to rob me of my peace.

Maybe you've heard those same comments that questioned your sanity and even your financial status, and you were more affected internally than you let on. It's easy to let those voices in even after decisions have been made. It's even easier to replay them during difficult moments at home when we question our own sanity for making the choice to follow God's call. *Did we hear Him wrong? Are they right?*

In a world that loves to make a clear division between mothers who work outside the home and those who don't, we are encouraged to pitch our tent on one side of the fence and camp there without ever considering what life looks like on the other side. You're on one side or the other. It's black or white; no gray allowed. Once you've moved from one side to the other, there's more that's lost or gained than just employment status. I noticed early on that there was little room given for conflicted emotions on either side of the fence.

Those I knew who stayed home were thrilled that I had the option to leave my career (and they assumed I felt the same and had no doubts), and those who worked assumed I was running toward an endless vacation with no misgivings about walking away from a career I cherished. It left me feeling like no one completely understood— and with an extra dose of shame and guilt that loved to taunt me in the quiet moments. What was wrong me with me? The reality was, I was going through a difficult transition, and instead of trying to grin and bear it, I needed to give myself grace to get through it.

If you're like me, you'd rather push through the discomfort of the unknown into the expected and known any day. It's hard to sit in the middle between what was and what is. It's harder still to articulate our feelings when those people around us are so sure of their own feelings about what we face. Comments like *Think of all the free time you'll have now* and *If I were home, I'd have such a clean house* do little to curb the voice within that struggles with what feels like a permanent and uncertain choice. We clearly remember (sometimes with more than one sigh) what it was like to have lunch breaks and a bathroom door that had no little fingers reaching beneath. We no longer have clearly established weekends or breaks to our day, and sometimes life feels like one long carousel ride that offers no pause to let us step off.

Just because society tries to place us at odds with working moms doesn't mean we have to go along with it. We need to be careful not to give in to temptation and glamorize the lives of our sisters working outside the home. We know what their day looks like because we once lived it, and we must resist the urge to focus only on the perks of working outside the home. We don't enjoy when others assume that we binge-watch TV all day, taking breaks only to get another cup of coffee and plan the next playdate. Likewise, we can't allow ourselves to make false assumptions about the lives working mothers lead. They deal with daily pressure that we don't have to face any longer, and we need to be sensitive to that as well.

Sure, they might assume that our days mimic theirs while on vacation, and there's probably a bit of truth in that if we are honest with ourselves. While we have the luxury of wearing whatever we feel like—or whatever is clean—they're buttoning and zipping themselves into clothes with buttons and zippers (the invention of the yoga capri is one way God has shown His love for me). Let's all take a moment of silence for those who wear heels instead of Skechers and slacks instead of yoga pants. Every morning they face an endless stream of activity. The stress of getting everyone ready for the day before walking through the doors of work has to be maddening—and they do this daily. They handle their babies and toddlers who cry at day care drop-off, face the unrelenting guilt of being unable to blow off work to stay with them, and deal with demanding bosses who are insensitive to the unique situations that a working mother experiences regularly. They come home to make dinner, do homework, bathe their children, and say goodnight—all without having a moment to breathe, much less take any time for themselves. Not to mention having a limited number of leave days to be home with kids who get sick at least once a month, being unable to attend school performances or events because of work, and being overlooked for promotions due to the inability to work the same overtime that childless colleagues do.

We face different battles, but we all battle.

It's a lot to handle, and our sisters raising children and working outside the home deserve our respect—and our offers of childcare when their sick leave inevitably runs out. It's no wonder at all that we are often the objects of envy from our working-mother friends. We face different battles, but we all battle. We can support one another instead of judging one another. Motherhood is hard for all of us, regardless of our employment status. We are held together by the bond of sleepless nights, T-shirts soaked with spit-up, and a fierce love for our children that rivals all others.

The Unexpected Changes

Unexpectedly, the transition to stay-at-home parenthood wreaks havoc on more than just your schedule and your ability to form an entire sentence without interruption. It changes relationships, sometimes irrevocably. Often, the relationships most altered are those you had with coworkers or colleagues—even though you swore nothing would change. Sometimes it's those with close friends who may or may not be mothers themselves.

I realized early in my days of being home that the support I yearned for from those I was once close to might not be given. Close relationships with longtime friends began to feel distanced. Things had changed. I had changed. There was no corner of my life that the broom of motherhood hadn't swept, and I was struggling to keep up with a life that I loved, but that I hardly recognized as my own. At the time it felt like another loss I wasn't prepared for, this unexpected loss of friendships.

There was no corner of my life that the broom of motherhood hadn't swept.

I felt left out and judged. I felt like I was too much or not enough: I was never able to feel completely comfortable in my own skin around my friends. I don't believe this was anyone's issue but my own, and it was simply part of the journey God took me on to find my true identity that I had overlooked along the way. Part of this discomfort comes from being alone with children for most of the day. Social skills and self-confidence decline rapidly when your most intellectual conversation is about who would win in an epic battle between Batman and Spider-Man. (It's definitely Spider-Man, by the way.)

I can see now that God was removing distractions from my life so that my focus could remain steadfast on Him. During the moments when I grieved the loss of these friends, there was a distinct tendency within myself to focus on specific moments in these relationships that perhaps I could have done differently to alter the outcome. Maybe I could have tried to be more like these mothers— and less like the one I had become. Perhaps you've been there too. Maybe you think, *Why can't I be more like her? She's so soft-spoken. My kids need a gentler mom.* Or *I wish I had her ability to deal with life so easily. She never really struggles with anything.* It's human nature to compare ourselves to others, but that doesn't make it a worthwhile activity.

Through every moment of doubt, I felt Jesus reassure me that this was my path in motherhood. I was the mom that I was, and it was who my kids needed me to be. My path wouldn't look like the others, but it was where He was leading. I couldn't deny that every decision I had made since becoming a mother felt led by the Holy Spirit, and I felt such peace with my decisions I could never truly question them. They all felt right. In the end, I had to sit with my grief for friendships lost and know there was a reason and purpose behind this new, albeit lonely, path.

Who you are now may be different from who you were then. This isn't a bad thing. In fact, if you're following Christ, you'll be constantly growing to become more like Him. This doesn't come without sacrifice, and it might cost you friendships that are holding you back, keeping you in old patterns and behaviors. Whom have you lost along the way? Who were you when you were with them? I know it's easier to focus on the loss of their love and support rather than on the gain of a closer relationship with Christ. You can't text Jesus to complain about not being able to find shorts shorter than Bermuda length but longer than you wore in high school. I get it. In these moments of loneliness, we can give God our sorrow for friends lost and trust that He will meet us in our pain.

When you are searching for the approval of anyone but God, the opinions of others have an opportunity to sink into places in your heart they were never meant to occupy. Off-handed comments and perceived disapprovals take up space in our minds and hearts where Jesus' truth is meant to be. In Christ, we are eternally approved, and we can know that this stamp of approval is unshakable. It does not fade with time, and it cannot be cut out of the eternal fabric our souls are made of. We will forever be God's daughters.

When we operate out of this knowledge—when we let it sink into the deepest corners of our stubborn and hesitant-to-really-believe-it hearts—we are no longer concerned with the fact that others may be talking about our parenting decisions, financial situation, or the behavior of our children. It is not our business. Our gaze is fixed upward, steady and unwavering, on the One who truly matters.

Yet we will still face comments that leave us mystified about how to respond: *I could never stay home with my kids. I'd go crazy!* Or *What about your degree? What a waste.* Or *You must have so much time to get things done!* Or, of course, *You'll go back to work once they're in school, right?* Sound familiar? Everyone has an opinion about your life, and sometimes it feels as though smiling and nodding would be much better replaced with a few curt words in response instead. It's so tempting to reply with snark instead of gentle truth, isn't it? Perhaps you're like me, and the perfect reply with just the right amount of biting sarcasm only comes to you hours later when it's too late to respond. This is probably for the best, and there have been numerous times I have thanked God for my slow SRS (Snark Response System).

When friends or even family question something so personal in your life, like the way your family operates, it's tempting to respond with defensiveness. There's always going to be that snide uncle who asks what you do all day or the former colleague who claims being home with her children would be a waste of her education—and drive her crazy. They might imagine that your life consists of end-less free time and sleeping in every morning, but you know the truth. Their flawed perception of your life is not your concern. A simple response of *It works for us!* suffices in most conversations—even when your preferred response includes the use of many words that are much more...shall we say, descriptive.

Surprisingly, the defensiveness and anger we feel in response to others sometimes comes from a place of guilt held deep within. When we've spent much of our lives working, it is incredibly easy to buy into the lie that we need to earn our keep and even the gift of being home with our children. If so many people wish to be in our very shoes, then shouldn't we at the very least earn the right to wear them?

My hope is that your spouse is supportive of your calling to be home with your children, but you should know that even with a supportive spouse, the temptation to feel guilty for staying home is still real. Sometimes the support from a hard-working spouse can exacerbate the feelings of guilt even more. For a long time I strug-gled with the fact that Ed spent his days working incredibly hard to enable me to enjoy the perks of being home. I constantly reminded myself of all of the working friends I had who were, at that very moment, earning an income for their families and proving them-selves an "equal" partner to their husbands. They were out working for a living while I was folding towels and wiping noses.

Subconsciously, I punished myself for not making a "real contri-bution" to our household. And I gave up reading—which I love! *If I can't sit down for an hour to read, then why bother? I should be spending the time reading to my kids anyway*, I'd think. I never thought about little things that might make my day go more smoothly or bring a smile to my face. I simply never thought about myself as anything other than a mother.

I believed that good moms focused only on their children and that the more I neglected myself for them, the more loved they would feel. As you can imagine, this made me extremely fun to live with. It turns out, never thinking about myself turned me into an incredibly selfish person who behaved very...selfishly. My attitude was consistently...shall we say, sour, and it was clear to the boys and Ed that I was always moody and exhausted.

I believed that good moms focused only on their children and that the more I neglected myself for them, the more loved they would feel.

I recently found, tucked in with some old papers, a handwritten list I wrote when Bryce was six months old. It was a weekly to-do list, sloppily written in pencil, that read: wash sippy cups, clean bathrooms, mop floors. I don't remember making this list, but I remember who I was when I made it. I can practically feel the pressure I placed on myself as I committed in writing that my house would be spotless. Clearly, at that moment in time, I couldn't give myself the grace I so desperately needed.

I hadn't yet found a comfortable rhythm to my days, and I longed for my work schedule of the past, so why not make a new one? Floors on Monday, bathrooms on Wednesday, and laundry on Friday. I'm still a stickler for a house that at least looks pulled together most days (because it makes me feel more relaxed and calm—and not because I put pressure on myself to keep it that way), but that schedule is long gone. My guess is that it only lasted a week or two before I threw in the dirty towel anyway. I've never been able to force myself to do certain chores on certain days for any length of time. It's not how I'm wired, though some days I wish I were.

Eventually, I shook myself free of the lie that the enemy had whispered in my ear that I needed to become worthy enough to earn this calling to be home with my kids. I allowed myself to enjoy my days, savor the moments with my children, and think about the future fun we would have together at home. I also began taking time to do my hair (goodbye ponytails 24-7). I researched hobbies. I began reading books, even if it was only in five-minute chunks. I embraced life.

Our role as mothers is a twenty-four-hour, seven-days-a-week calling that requires more of us than any other role in our lives ever will. So wear those lounge pants. Enjoy that cup of coffee at 9. And 10. And 11. Make yourself a cup of tea and have a cookie. Take a midday walk with the kids and call a friend. Denying yourself the perks of staying home only makes for a grumpy and bitter mother—whom no one wants to be at home with. There is freedom in Jesus—and also in the waistband of good yoga pants—so embrace both.

Your perception of your role in both your family and your home changes everything. When you can embrace the incredible responsibility and also the freedom you've been given, you can begin to step into the life God is calling you to with all of its beauty and difficulties. When others offer comments like *Must be nice* and *I wish I could stay home*, you'll be able to honestly reflect a spirit of genuine gratitude instead of feeling guilt and shame.

It *is* nice, and you *are* thankful it's the life you get to live. Every day I feel an enormous sense of gratitude that I've never felt forced to leave my children to go to work. Some of you have been on both sides of this: You've been both a working mom and a stay-at-home mom. If you've done both, then you understand in a way I cannot the struggles that working moms face every day. While we all know that work may provide a sense of escape that we long for during this transition, the benefits of being home are numerous when we really consider them.

I've been given the immense privilege of spending my days snuggling my children, watching them learn and grow, and growing closer to God while doing so. Is there a greater gift for a mother than to be there for her children every step of the way? It's exhausting and exhilarating. It's all the things that every mother knows motherhood to be. And at the end of every day (even the ones when I'm doubting my own sanity and cleaning ketchup out of the dog's fur), I'm simply astonished at God's mercy in allowing this to be my life.

Beyond your clothing choices (comfort is always key in the land of the living-room dweller), it is absolutely normal during this season of life to feel misunderstood by those you once felt close to. God has a way of doing work within us without providing a warning to those we are in relationship with. Our decisions may come as a surprise to them, but we are following God's lead, and that is typically a personal path, not one broadcast to the masses. It is not your responsibility to provide a backstory as to why you have chosen to stay home/homeschool/breastfeed/formula feed/etc. unless you feel like you want to. All of that is between you, your spouse, and Jesus. Your opinionated Aunt Lorraine will have to accept that.

Instead of telling those people with their critical words or raised eyebrows what you are tempted to say (we all know what you'd like to say!), take it to Jesus Himself. He's had ample experience with those closest to Him questioning who He really is. He understands feelings of betrayal and sorrow. Your anger and frustration are not a surprise to Him, and He wants to take those feelings from you and replace them with peace.

Jesus isn't the only One who experienced the criticism of those closest to Him. Perhaps you might relate to a maidservant named Hagar, who bore a child with Sarah's husband, Abraham, when Sarah grew tired of waiting for God's promise of a child of her own. Once Hagar became pregnant, Sarah's feelings toward her changed significantly, and she only wanted Hagar gone. Perhaps she became a glaring reminder of Sarah's impatience with God and the consequences of her unbelief. Hagar experienced firsthand what it means to no longer feel included and worthy.

Hagar's name for God was *El Roi*, which means "You Are the God Who Sees." God spoke to Hagar when she fled Sarah's harsh treatment and promised to multiply her descendants. She was not unknown to Him, though she felt insignificant because of her circumstances. Although she was now excluded from where she was once welcomed, Hagar knew that if she still had God, she had the only thing that mattered.

When we experience the negative emotions of others, we have to remember that it is not about us. When our focus remains on our relationship with Jesus and the mission He's given us in our everyday lives, we no longer need to feel excluded or as if we need to prove anything to anyone. The voice of Christ must be louder than anything and anyone else we listen to.

How do you and I hear God when the voices of others threaten to drown Him out? To start, you'll need to get comfortable being quiet within yourself, silencing those voices that tell you what you're doing doesn't matter and isn't important. Ignore the ones saying the dishes in the sink really need to be done right this minute. Give yourself permission to just let those things go. You're a daughter of God. What else really matters right now?

When you are quiet before your heavenly Father, that's all there is. There's you, there's God, and there's the breath that enters and leaves your body that is given only by Him. Everything and everyone else is peripheral, not your concern. It's just a girl and her Father. When your heart is postured in humility with anticipation of what He will do, He will not leave you waiting. He will always answer even if His answer is simply to sit with you in the quiet, being together.

> *There's you, there's God, and there's the breath that enters and leaves your body that is given only by Him.*

He knows your life well. He knows this isn't easy for you. He also knows that He has exactly what you seek, and your efforts to find it elsewhere will be fruitless. Rather than try to correct the misperceptions of others about your life at home, it is far easier to agree that life at home with your children really is a blessing. We get a front-row seat to all of the glory and chaos of childhood, and the moments with our children are cherished (not every moment— let's not be ridiculous—no one cherishes the memory of a tantrum in the toy aisle). Still, you have been pulled away from your career into this life for a reason. If you are open to hearing it, there's a message for you in this season.

What I Learned in Sunday School

When I was four, I went to Sunday school with my cousins at their evangelical church. My father is Catholic, and for the majority of my childhood when we attended church, we went to Catholic mass, so this was quite different for me. I remember sitting at a long table with all the other children as we made a simple craft. The cloud was made of two pieces of construction paper, stapled around the edges and filled with stuffing. We stapled rainbow-colored crepe paper streamers to the bottom, and the Sunday school teacher wrote "God Is Love" across the cloud with a black permanent marker.

I took the craft home, and my parents hung it on my bedroom wall next to my bed. It hung on my wall until we moved when I was thirteen. Throughout the years I glanced up at it, with its faded and torn streamers, and read over and over the words *God Is Love*. Looking back, I rarely attended any kind of church program for children, yet on one of the few occasions that I went, the only and the best message I could have received was given to me.

Clearly, when God has a message to send, He will go to great lengths to make sure it is received. What might He be trying to communicate to you during this time at home when your patience runs out before nine in the morning and the work feels endless? Who are those friends or family members in your life who have given you support in this process? In the beginning, when this life-change of staying home is new, it might feel as though everyone has deserted you or that true and honest support is hard to find. Rather than place your focus on the negative voices (including the one within), take a moment and ask God to bring to mind those people in your life whose presence has been one of peace, not judgment or drama.

My Aunt Patty, for instance, has been an unending source of support for me during some of the roughest moments of life at home with little ones. She, too, left a career to be home with her three (now adult) boys, and hers is often the reassuring voice that reminds me that not only is it hard work, but that she *gets it*. She validates my emotions without an ounce of judgment. It's a breath of fresh air when tantrums or whining leave me breathless. We all need someone on our side who, as we navigate the waves, stands at the shore and cheers us on. Someone who can promise that it gets easier and that we aren't alone.

I also have a handful of girlfriends who have stuck with me through every life change. They're the ones who cheered me on when I—with tears—resigned, who text randomly even after months of busyness to check in, and who have been nothing but supportive as I began following my dream of writing.

A couple of them were teacher colleagues of mine, and when they stuck by my side through everything without reservation, it meant the world to me. They called me to hang out when they had Christmas or summer vacation—they did what they could, when they could. These are the types of friendships and relationships I encourage you to remind yourself of when you begin to feel alone or judged.

And if you didn't happen to keep friendships from your previous career, don't shame yourself for it. Sometimes it is impossible to weather a storm and keep the entire crew aboard until you reach land. It's inevitable you'll lose some friends along the way. Rest assured, God knows what we need in every season of life, and new friendships may be right around the corner. Your loneliness and the isolation you feel are not unseen by God. After all, He is *El Roi*, The God Who Sees.

Before we end, a quick note about forgiveness: I truly believe that relationships are needlessly damaged when we don't take the time to think of another's perspective. As you walk through your feelings with the Lord, take a moment to ask Him to show you where a shift in perspective might allow you to understand how someone's hurtful comments could have been misconstrued or received through a biased lens.

While it is increasingly easy to find reasons to be offended in this world, as Christ-followers and cheek-turners, we can't be among those looking for ways to be offended. Walking through life in a defensive stance leaves no room for humility. Jesus heard it all. He was accused of being the enemy, yet He responded not in anger, but with reasoning and a gentle spirit. We can do the same when someone questions our work in the home and the way we serve our families. We can forgive, move on, and grow because the One who is in us is greater than he who is in the world.

> *As Christ-followers and cheek-turners,
> we can't be among those looking for ways
> to be offended.*

You know the importance of this work you're doing for your family. You don't need others to validate that you are worthy of the gift of being home. Let's embrace our blessings and own them, knowing that our Father is the God Who Sees and that He sees us for who we really are. We don't have to let anything else but the peace of God settle into our hearts because that's exactly what they are meant to hold. Own your blessings. After all, the chubby fingers reaching under the bathroom door *are* pretty adorable.

Reflection Questions:

1. Whose approval do you seek the most? Family? Friends? God? Why?

2. When others ask questions and make assumptions about your choice to be home, what emotion do you feel the most? With what words would you like to respond to that question?

3. When you have felt insignificant, how has God shown you that He sees you?

⟶ Talk to Him About It

Lord, help me to hear Your voice above all others. Remind me that pleasing You is what matters, not what others think. Guard my tongue when I'm tempted to respond to others with words that don't honor You. Thank You for the gift of Your love and for being the God Who Sees. I trust You, Father. Amen.

Good Grief

Why You Need to Grieve During Change

*Grief is in two parts. The first is loss. The
second is the remaking of life.*
Anne Roiphe[2]

Jen, do you think there's a reason you keep getting rejections from the work-from-home jobs you've applied for?" my friend asked gently over the phone one afternoon.

My reply came out in broken sobs as I came face-to-face with what I knew but had denied for so long: God wanted my complete attention, and He would not allow a new job to distract me from the important growth I needed to experience.

During the anguished period of time when I was determined to run from the difficult truths that haunted me, and I applied for work-from-home jobs like a crazy woman, my emotions took a backseat to all else. Who wants to take time out to grieve or feel any kind of sadness? I was too busy trying to replace what I felt had been lost—and what I was owed for all my work and effort.

I convinced myself a job was to help our family out financially even though the income wasn't truly needed. Sure, extra money would have been a huge help to our little family as we tried to minimize extras and watched our bank account closely. But God was providing enough for us to have exactly what we needed—no more, no less. Secretly, I thought about how great it would feel to go shopping with *my* money instead of feeling as though I was taking from the family budget to buy myself fancy shampoo or expensive makeup (even though if I had bought those things for myself with family money, it wouldn't have been an issue or even a topic of discussion).

There was so much pride involved in my quest to find a job that I couldn't even see the sin in it. Getting a job had simply become a goal, and I always met my goals. So when God drew a firm line in the sand and said no, I felt more than just disappointment. His instruction was a direct blow to my pride. During that call with my friend, I finally lost all willpower to continue believing the lies I told myself about my true motivation to find work. The flood of tears that flowed during that conversation was the healing balm I needed to move past the stumbling block of my pride.

Sometimes a tearful conversation with a close friend can pave the way for healing that you aren't aware you need. I ended the call feeling a sense of relief. I no longer felt a need to defiantly continue striving to find work. I now could accept God's answer and settle into the work on the soul that awaited me.

Have you ever been there? Running from God, fists pumping through the air? Even though you know it's a race you'll never win, it feels like there's too much ground behind you to stop. When we run this kind of unwinnable race, it's tempting to imagine that God chases after us, angry and red-faced—not to mention annoyed at our disobedience. But we serve a God who is abundant in mercy and slow to anger. I often consider my mother's heart to be a miniscule version of God's heart for us. When your children disobey or struggle to believe that your limits are what's best, do you lash out in anger? Most likely you see through their tears and anger right into their hearts that are broken and unaware of your knowledge and concern for their well-being. I believe it's the same with our Father in heaven. He knows that our tears and anger are part of the process, and instead of chasing after us red-faced and angry, He simply runs next to us with His arms open and waiting to embrace us.

Grief is intrinsic to any transition. People, though, rarely speak of it. We'd rather focus on the highs of life and sweep the lows under the bed with the dust bunnies that taunt us when we search for the lost remote control. Maybe you are experiencing the grief that comes with letting go of your job title or the dreams for yourself you were sure would have come true by this point in life, but the feelings behind letting go are the same.

Where is God in all of this? you might wonder. If He knows your heart, then He should know how much this hurts, right? In my darkest moments of struggling to find peace while settling into life at home, I wondered why He wouldn't pull me out of the funk I found myself in. If it was His will for me to stay home, then why did I feel so empty? I was so excited to have the time with my son. It felt like a dream come true in so many ways, yet there was this nagging sense of loss. I loved my child so deeply, but I couldn't shake this sense of sadness. Surely this wasn't the abundant life Jesus said He came to give me. So where was it?

When the train of transition pulls into your station, you can be sure that grief is riding as an unknown hitchhiker, sometimes sitting in the last car you'd expect. When Ed and I got married, we had dated almost five years. During those five years we had experienced our share of difficulty and felt more than prepared to become husband and wife. Through every high and low, our commitment to one another was cemented, and there was no doubt on our wedding day that we were meant to be together.

We had a beautiful wedding and planned to leave on our honeymoon three days later. Imagine my surprise when, packing for our honeymoon a couple days after our wedding, I began to cry inexplicably. Ed was concerned, of course, and asked what was wrong. All I could really say was that I felt like everything was changing. I felt a loss that I couldn't explain, and I felt sad that I was no longer my parents' daughter, or a friend to my friends, in the way that I had been just a few days before. I was now a wife, and my priorities had forever been changed.

Of course this change was good, but I still needed to grieve this transition. It didn't mean that I didn't love my husband or feel fully committed to our new life together. I wholeheartedly embraced my new title as his wife, but the woman I left behind also needed the proper send-off—and my emotions were intent on making sure she received one. Stepping from one role to another doesn't always feel like a clean break from the old into the new. The step can feel messy and painful, but those feelings don't mean the step is wrong or bad. Growth comes with growing pains, and the growth you experience as you accept the call of God to be home with your children is no different.

This might not come as welcome news, especially if you're accustomed to sprinting past sadness in an effort to "stay positive." The fear of experiencing emotions other than happiness is not rare. No one likes to anticipate that grief is around the corner—or admit that it's sitting beneath a shaking smile that threatens to fall. The truth is, though, that—like most things in life—the anticipation of pain is often worse than the pain itself. We don't need to fear its arrival; we only need to rest in the fact that Jesus provides for us during the lows of life just as much as He does during the highs. He's there, smack-dab in the middle of the pain, providing ever-present comfort to soften the hardest blows we experience. Nothing is hopeless with Jesus. Nothing.

The emotions I felt mere days after my wedding were necessary in order for me to fully step into my new role as a wife. Once I allowed the inevitable grief from the transition from fiancée to wife to express itself, I was then free to enjoy our honeymoon and newlywed days in the ways I had always dreamed I would. How then can we expect to step into the role of being a stay-at-home parent without similar emotions coming to the surface? Even if you didn't particularly enjoy your job, the lack of its presence in your life will create a striking difference in the way you spend your days. You've lost not just a place to go every day to use the bathroom alone. You've lost daily interaction with an entire community.

Motherhood itself changes a woman in countless ways. We aren't just growing our families; we are growing ourselves. It's more than just jeans that fit a bit more snugly and a few well-earned bags appearing under our eyes. Ask any father, and he will tell you that the mother of his children is not the woman she was before she traded dinners and dancing for diapers and dishes. The grief you may be feeling might be more related to the transition to motherhood than to giving up your career—and that is completely acceptable and normal. If you've walked away from a career right as you walked into motherhood, as I did, the two transitions can become impossibly interwoven, creating one enormous pile of...stuff to work through. As mothers, we want not only to do it all and have it all, but we want to be perfect through it all too.

The process of pregnancy, giving birth, and instantly becoming a mother is much like a sort of internal whiplash. You can read every book that's been written describing the process, but until you're in it, you'll never fully understand. The foreign weight of responsibility for the very life of another human is daunting and anxiety provoking. As much as we love our babies, our bodies and souls have gone through a whole lot to bring another human into the world—and no matter how easy your delivery was, there's no denying the impact this life-changing event has made.

I vividly remember the days following the birth of Bryce. There was this moment, the morning after we brought him home from the hospital, when he was lying on the bed in front me in all of his newborn frog-legged glory. His tiny feet still wrinkled and purple-tinged, he lay there gazing up at me in what seemed to be wonder. In that moment, as I looked into his eyes, the full weight and beauty of motherhood barreled toward me at full speed. He was mine. When I dressed him in an outfit that only days before seemed too small to hold anything but a doll, I felt dancing within me the unfettered joy of having a child to call my own. I would never be the same again, and the woman I had been before birth felt like a blurred memory at best. Everything was irrevocably changed in a moment. It felt beautifully terrifying.

I often think about the way God has chosen to bring children into the world. He could have chosen any way, but He chose this one. For months, we experience the growth and pain that come with preparing for a baby before we receive the complete joy of a baby to love—and it is through this incredible experience that we give birth to a new version of ourselves. We come out of the birth experience often feeling empowered: We survived a sort of pain we never knew existed, and we persevered. Only in the days and months after the birth does the true growth of motherhood begin. In the endless giving of ourselves for another, the broken finds its way to becoming beautiful. In the laying down of our lives, over and over again we become closer to Christ's example than ever.

If you've just had a baby, you might feel more broken than beautiful in this moment—and that's perfectly normal and expected. There's good reason to feel the way you do. Maybe you, like I once did, feel the need to get every detail just right—so you don't mess up this whole mothering thing, and your baby someday tells a therapist about the way you never mastered perfecting the latch during breastfeeding. This adjustment to being a mom is so hard, isn't it? And sometimes—for me, at least—my transition to motherhood looked a lot like frustration and even anger.

I lashed out at my husband and was short with just about anyone who tried to help. I can see now that I was dealing with a bit more than just the hormonal shift of motherhood: I was experiencing postpartum depression and anxiety. My symptoms weren't the typical ones you see advertised. I had no trouble getting out of bed or taking care of my baby, but there was an undercurrent of frustration and fear that plagued me. I learned that emotions and experiences after birth are so unique to each of us that anything out of line with typical highs and lows is deserving of a closer look. If that's you, too, and life feels a bit heavier or different than usual, I encourage you to speak with your doctor. Your body is struggling to find balance again, and there's no shame in getting help. You'll find the way back to yourself again. It just takes time—and is no reflection of your ability as a mother or of the depth of your love for your baby. It's okay to need help and to go find it. It takes immense courage.

Contributing to the stress of being a mom, however old your kids, is our striving for a perfection we were never meant to strive for. When He sees His daughters, especially those fresh into motherhood, working toward the impossible, God must grieve. Our bodies are nearly broken (they feel as though they've been totaled), our brains are on overdrive trying to remember all the things we now have to remember, and our hearts—which God knows—are shattered by an overflowing love, concern, and adoration for our child that no one ever warned us about.

I remember, several times during those early days of motherhood, falling asleep with Bryce in my arms—and waking because I couldn't remember where I had put him down. I was suffering from severe exhaustion that seemed to have no end in sight.

Once a baby is in the equation, our lives no longer feel as though they are our own. Add to new motherhood the loss of a career and a misplaced sense of worth, and the table that held up your sense of normalcy finally collapses beneath the weight of your grief. Each factor is enough on its own to bring upheaval, but when combined, they're enough to make us desperate to find anything that reminds us of who we used to be.

The monotonous repetition that motherhood brings makes life unrecognizable, and it's easy to feel as though who you used to be is now a figure walking in fog. The shape is vaguely familiar, but the rest is too muted to make out. Suddenly the simple things we used to enjoy feel frivolous in the face of surviving each day in this new world of burping and swaddling.

Sometimes we need a reminder of who we still are, and it can arrive in the most unexpected of ways. In the days following Bryce's birth, I was experiencing the exhaustion and endless cycle of newborn care that most new mothers experience. Friends and family came to visit, and it felt a bit like an out-of-body experience. I was me—but not me. I was this new version of myself, a mom. The anticipated being I held within me was suddenly separate from me, but still so intimately connected. He was mine and I was his—all of me was his, with none to spare for anyone else. Motherhood had swallowed me whole.

Overnight, literally, my life was unrecognizable. A friend of mine—who was a new mom herself—brought muffins and a celebrity gossip magazine and left them at my doorstep with a sweet note. A gift for me that wasn't about nursing or baby care! It felt like a flashback to who I had been a week before, and it reminded me of who I still was.

This gift was all I needed to know that I would adjust and that life would feel normal again. Even though motherhood was front and center in this moment, there was still room for who I was. I didn't have to forfeit everything I used to enjoy in order to be a good mother. I doubt that my friend knew her simple gift would communicate so much more than she intended, but in the years since I've been profoundly grateful for her thoughtfulness. We all need a friend like that—and we all need to be that friend.

Even though motherhood was front and center in this moment, there was still room for who I was.

We need to remember the things we once enjoyed before our eyes looked weary and our hands were cracked and dry from wiping and washing. When the woman you once were—or thought you would be—is nowhere to be found, it's easy to give in to two feelings: guilt and fear.

You might feel guilt because you assume if you loved your children enough, you wouldn't feel this way. If you willingly made the choice to give up your career, you probably wonder if grief should even be a part of this journey. No one forced you to stay home with your children, and there's probably a voice in your head taunting you for daring to complain about the blessed life that you lead. My inner voice used to say something like *Isn't this what you always wanted? You're ungrateful. Most mothers would give anything to be home with their kids. What's your problem?*

The truth is that parenthood, in any form, is hard. Perhaps you made the transition to stay-at-home motherhood a few years after your children were born. You tried the working mom way of life, and this is where you feel called to be in this season. For some of you, adoption may have been the road you walked to motherhood, and staying home with your new child is necessary for a multitude of reasons. Regardless of what led you to this place, grace is the answer. You would never tell your best friend that she must not love her children if she feels grief over what her life used to look like, so don't speak so harshly to yourself either. Give yourself the grace you give to others.

You may also feel fear because you worry that life will never be the same again. The foundation for this fear is not necessarily that life has been irrevocably changed, but that your happiness and contentment with life are gone forever. *What if it always feels this way? What if I never settle into the contented routine that others seem to? Was this a huge mistake? Do I just not have the stay-at-home-mom gene?* The questions and fears that love to taunt you do not have their roots in truth. They find their power in your own emotions and reactions to the thoughts themselves. You have what it takes to be content in this life you have been led to. Remember Paul's words about his learning to be content in all circumstances? You can do it too. It simply requires a complete dependence on Christ. Is this possible? Absolutely.

Contentment will require you to embrace—at your core, not just mentally—the truth of who you are in Christ. We love to say that we know the love of Jesus and that we derive our worth from Him alone—but in the deepest spaces of our soul, do we actually believe He loves us? However strong our belief in God's love for us is or isn't, the inevitable grief that comes with change may make us doubt His love. We may quietly begin to jog away from the pain before we begin an all-out race of avoidance. Even the best changes bring some degree of grief as we embrace the new and release the old.

Three years ago my family experienced a wonderful change, but my heart still experienced grief within the joy. I remember how I tearfully kissed Bryce goodbye as I left for the hospital to give him the brother I was hoping he would (eventually) love. Lucky enough to experience something called prodromal labor, I had labored for the three days prior. "Do you think this is it?" I'd ask Ed as I rubbed my lower back and breathed through each contraction only to have them fade away to nothing within a few hours. The next day would then be a cruel repeat of the previous one. I was beginning to wonder if I knew my own body as well as I thought I did. Active labor felt like it was playing hard to get, and I was getting more and more frustrated.

Throughout my pregnancy with Bradley, I was laser-focused on giving Bryce a sibling—something I didn't experience for myself until I was nearly eleven. I wanted him to have everything that I missed as a child: family vacations with someone sharing the backseat while we drove, holidays with someone else opening toys, and weekends spent together as a family without the need to invite a friend over to play. I knew that it wouldn't always be as wonderful as I hoped (during my own playdates as a girl, I had seen enough sibling interactions to know that much), but I longed for our family to include more than one child in a way that I'm not sure all mothers do. So that evening, when the contractions refused to fade, I knew that it was finally time to kiss my first boy goodbye for a short while (oh, how I hoped short!) and say hello to our second.

In that moment, when I kissed Bryce's forehead, framed with curls, I knew that I was, in fact, kissing our existing family goodbye and stepping into the place where a new one awaited. For nine months my body had held our precious son, and it was time for the birth of the baby and this new season of life. Walking from the playroom where Bryce played with my parents and into the garage, I allowed the tears to fall to my cheeks as I straddled two worlds, two families.

On the other side of the door that closed behind me was everything I knew and loved, and hurt to leave: I knew that when I returned, our lives and our family would be forever changed. All of the days spent at the zoo as a threesome and the evenings spent together, just the three of us, played like a movie reel through my mind. This time in our lives was all going to be a memory now. Throughout my second pregnancy I struggled to imagine how I could love another baby the way I loved Bryce, but I knew that, somehow, my heart would grow right along with our family. I was so excited to become a family of four with two sons I could hardly stand it—or the overwhelming hip and back pain of the third trimester.

In that moment at the door, though, the grief was real. It was real and valid, a side effect of the transition a soul must go through to welcome anything new and vibrant. When the old must go or die—it feels like a death—grieving, however that may look for you, is required. We can sweep it under the rug of our souls and say we are fine. In fact, that's the preferred method for so many of us. The problem with this method is, I believe, unless the old is truly dealt with, it will dampen the joy of the new in unexpected ways.

Had I forced myself to grin through those last moments with my son as an only child, even when I was alone with Ed on the way to the hospital, I believe it would have come with a cost. Would I really have been ready to welcome my new baby?

Bradley was born in a chaotic delivery room with only a nurse present to deliver him. All of those days spent in fruitless labor were redeemed as he made his debut in a lightning-fast delivery. The moment he was born, with Ed begging me to open my eyes that were clenched tightly in pain, I felt the true joy that comes with birth. How is it that pain and joy are so tightly interwoven that we can experience them in the same moment? In the dimly lit and quiet hours after meeting Bradley for the first time, I felt my heart double in size. He was six pounds of glorious joy. I held him as he quietly yawned, sighed, and gently stretched in my arms just as he had within me just hours before. My eyes intently gazed at his face in wonder. He was an incredibly beloved son, loved just as much as the first.

I believe that because I felt the grief in the moments leading up to my second birth—I welcomed it even—when Bradley was born, I was able to not only embrace him mind, body, and soul, but I was able to do so with serenity and peace, the byproducts of allowing grief to move through the soul during transition.

Have you ever cried over something and thought yourself silly for it? *I'm just over-emotional. My period is due. Why am I crying over this?* Perhaps the loss of your place in the working world feels like it isn't worth grieving over. Especially if being home is something you've *chosen.* Tears are important, though. There is a reason God has given us this way of expressing our deepest sorrow. When Lazarus died, Jesus knew He was going to raise His friend to life once again. And yet, the Bible tells us, Jesus wept. Biblical scholars have speculated about the reason behind the tears of Christ, but that's not what I want to focus on now.

If we look at the information we are given—Jesus wept—those two words give us all we need to draw a conclusion we can trust: Grief matters. Not only does grief matter, but it serves an important purpose. Tears have value in God's economy. The Bible is perfect—nothing can be added or extracted from it to improve it—so if the fact that Christ wept real tears has been included, we know it is there for a reason. We aren't to hold tears back when they threaten to fall. We are surely no stronger than Christ. If we feel the need to grieve with tears, then we must honor our soul's desire to release the pain in this way. It is a gift from God that we have the ability to do so.

As you've probably figured out by now, most of the best things in life require some work—among those things, experiencing the joy that lives just on the other side of grief. Understanding your worth in Christ and grieving the loss of what you've left behind might not get dirt under your fingernails, but it will still be work. Important work. We can believe in God with a faith that's stronger than any other and at the same time ignore who we are in Him.

It is easier to focus on who God is than who we are *in* Him and *to* Him. He is mighty, omnipotent, eternal, and holy. Who are you, then, in the shadow of such greatness? You are made righteous in Christ, beloved, forgiven, and set free. Don't allow your insecurity to rob you of your true identity. You aren't your career or credentials. Those are things of this world that will fade away. Your soul knows the truth at its core.

> *You are made righteous in Christ,*
> *beloved, forgiven, and set free.*

My boys love the Disney movie *Moana*. The scene at the very end—when Moana is bravely walking toward the volcanic demon Te Ka, who once was Te Fiti, and sings, *This does not define you, this is not who you are, you know who you are*—makes me tear up every time. My emotional reaction to the scene goes much deeper than the images on the screen. We define ourselves by so much—by our failures, our losses, the worst parts of ourselves—yet, Christ reminds us that none of it defines us...because of Him. We know who we are:

We are His. We belong to the God of the universe, and we are royalty because of His great mercy. We can't let ourselves get lost in the details that don't matter—and it's all details. We are His. Let's rest in that and *let it go*. (Enough with the Disney, I know.)

Facing Grief in All Its Goodness

Back to grief and why it's good. The thing about grief is that it tends to fade when we don't deny its presence and instead face it head-on. Throughout the journey, motherhood brings the opportunity for growth through grief. One after another there will be moments that feel bittersweet, and though our tendency is often to try to sidestep the hard feelings that arise, the best thing to do is to unflinchingly face them head-on. At first this approach seems counterintuitive, but once you experience the power of welcoming emotion and allowing it to pass through you, the process of healthy grieving will become easier to repeat.

A few months ago I made an announcement to Ed and the boys. "It's time to get rid of all of these baby things," I said with determination in my voice.

I had put our baby furniture, infant bouncers, high chair, and breast pump in a corner of the one-time nursery. "We'll have a yard sale—recoup some of the costs," I explained.

Ed agreed that it was time, and the boys were excited to have a yard sale where they might make some money of their own selling old toys. I posted a yard sale ad online for the following weekend. We were all set, and I bought poster board to make signs advertising the sale to hang around town.

The evening before the sale, as we sat at the table having dinner, I glanced at the tile floor between my chair and Ed's. I remembered how—and it seemed like yesterday—the infant bouncer had sat there with a two-week-old Bryce in it, watching us eat dinner as he squirmed in his footed sleeper. I burst into tears, startling Ed and the boys.

"I can't do it, honey. I can't sell this stuff. It's *too soon*," I sobbed. It wasn't a gentle shedding of tears. It was a full-on ugly cry. My shoulders shook with sobs while my family looked on in stunned silence.

"Apparently," Ed said, trying not to laugh. I began to laugh through my tears and reassured the boys that I was fine.

"You must really love that baby stuff, Mom," Bryce said.

I explained that it wasn't the stuff at all, but the memories the stuff held that I was struggling to let go of. My tears were a response to a time in my life that I couldn't get back—a time in their lives, too, that was gone forever. We ended up calling off the yard sale. I couldn't imagine that anyone would want to buy baby items from a sobbing seller, and I knew I needed to be gentle with myself and my grieving process. Once I faced my emotions instead of bulldozing my way ahead without acknowledging them, I felt as though my soul had experienced its own decluttering—even though our baby gear still sat in the corner of the nursery.

God has given us the gift of tears to provide an emotional cleansing. It's a way to allow our bodies and souls to process emotion as one. The opportunities to work through grief and to experience growth during motherhood are never-ending. Four nights ago, Bradley pulled away from my breast during our bedtime nursing session and whispered, "I can't get da milk out." It was confirmation of what I already suspected. My breast milk was dwindling to the point of drying up.

My nursing experience with both of my boys had a rocky beginning. The early days after birth—waiting for my milk to come in and feeling the toe-curling pain every time the baby's latch was wrong—remain fresh in my mind. I met with lactation consultants and showed them my scabbed nipples. I left any sort of vanity at the door because I desperately wanted to know how to nourish my babies through breastfeeding. Once my babies and I learned how to do the nursing thing, though, we were off and running. And we ran—for a long, long time. After over three years of stroking his curls away from his sweaty forehead while he nursed, I thought I would be more than ready to close this chapter of our relationship.

Instead, I found myself allowing the tears to fall and processing my grief the way that has always led to healing for me: writing. I wrote Bradley a letter, telling him about all the things I loved about nursing him and all the things I would miss. I imagine that years from now he might find it a bit odd that his mother wrote him a letter commemorating her nursing experience, but I'm willing to bet that if he has children by that point, his wife will understand completely. Motherhood hurts. It hurts in beautiful and aching ways we never anticipated when we were pregnant and only feared the pain of labor.

Embracing the Broken Things

A few weeks ago Ed and I sat with the boys around our backyard firepit making s'mores. With nights like the one we were having set firmly in his mind, Ed built the firepit himself, working tirelessly to prepare the ground and build the pit brick by brick. That evening, we made s'more after s'more and enjoyed the quiet popping of the campfire. Bradley wanted yet another, and we gave him one more with the assurance that it was his last for the night. (I was already pondering if a child sick from too much sugar was in my future.)

Bradley looked down at his last s'more, gooey with melted marshmallow and chocolate, and furrowed his little brow. "I don't like this one. It's broken," he said.

I glanced down and saw that the top graham cracker was cracked, but the marshmallow was working like glue to hold it on top. "It's still just as good broken," I replied.

He pondered my words for a moment and, with a slight smile, flipped over the s'more and said, "I'll eat it this way then."

As I watched him eat his treat, I thought to myself how many times I've flipped over a broken thing in my own life to hide the cracks. How many times have I smiled and replied, "I'm great!" when a friend asked how I was? I might have covered over the cracks with a smile—flipped my own brokenness over to hide it—but what did I gain from doing so? What if I had shared the truth or, at the very least, not worked so hard to hide it?

We live in a society that loves to focus solely on the brighter side of life. We love to watch TV shows about renovating homes, taking the broken, and producing unbelievable beauty within a 30-minute time span. No one wants to sit in the broken for long without seeing some sort of improvement on the horizon. When we allow ourselves to sit in the broken—in the places within that haven't produced beauty yet—and invite God to sit with us, He begins to do the work only He can do. In this honest and broken place, in the depths of our pain, we can see that He is there with us, and He is working.

No one wants to sit in the broken for long.

At this point you might be fearful if you allow yourself to acknowledge the grief that accompanies life changes, good or bad, you will simply wallow in it without any relief in sight. I can tell you from experience the opposite happens. Once you've accepted those feelings of sorrow, it provides an opportunity for the healing of God to take place—for Him to bind up your wounds and create the new thing He's wanted to make within you all along.

Now, I would be remiss in a chapter about grief if I didn't say a word or two about depression. Life change comes with grief, yes, but there is a point in which the grief becomes constant, overwhelming, or seemingly endless. In that case, you might need to consider that something other than transitional grief is at play. I've experienced both depression and anxiety at different points in my life, and I can say with confidence that I know myself well enough to know the difference between a grief that moves through me and a cloud of depression that hovers above unyieldingly. If you feel you might be experiencing the latter, I encourage you to seek help. Those of us on the other side of the clouds that threaten to overtake your joy and zest for life have found that there is a clear and marked difference between the two forms of grief, and it is worth seeking help for depression. There is no shame in taking medication, supplements, and/or talking to a professional. Christ heals today through these very channels.

Coming face-to-face with sadness is uncomfortable at first—and you might not even be sure how to access your own feelings of grief. Prayer is always a good place to start. After all, Christ has been watching you throughout this process, and He knows what you need before you even ask. Be honest with Him, and ask Him to reveal in you the places that need healing that you may not be aware of. Journaling can also help reveal things you've kept hidden to yourself and provide a place to process and evaluate your inner state of being.

Above all, whatever emotion presents itself, take it to Jesus. He's been waiting and watching, hoping that you would lift your eyes to Him. He wants to give you freedom and faith instead of fear, joy instead of mourning. Accept His gifts and walk freely into this new season of growth that awaits you.

⟿ Reflection Questions

1. What place of hidden grief in your life, if any, is waiting to be acknowledged?

2. What scares you most about allowing yourself to experience the grief that comes even in joyful transitions?

3. Which transitions in motherhood bring you the most grief?

⟿ Talk to Him About It

Father, I bring my aching heart to You. I ask that You would show me my own brokenness, so that I can offer it to You for healing. Help me to face the grief that is hidden from others, but not from You. Walk beside me, Lord, as I wade through waters that feel too deep to cross alone. I trust You, Father. Amen.

More Than Motherhood

Why Parenthood Is Not Enough

*Be who God meant you to be and
you will set the world on fire.*
St. Catherine of Siena[3]

Sunlight streamed through the living room as I sat on the couch, my Bible open on my lap. I bowed my head in silent prayer and asked God to give me something—anything—that would renew a sense of joy in my heart.

I was feeling run-down and burned out. I loved my boys fiercely, but outside of the love I had for them and Ed, I felt empty. I wanted something just for me, but I couldn't pinpoint what I needed.

The weekend before I had sat on a stool in a coffee shop and tearfully told my friend about the emptiness I felt. We talked about my new camera and my love of writing, and I felt the tiniest inkling of joy start to edge its way back into me. I still wasn't sure what I should do, but I left our meeting feeling hopeful that there was something out there for me. She told me to ask God to give me something, to show me what I should do that would be serving Him and fulfilling to me.

During all of the times I felt this emptiness, it never occurred to me to ask God to provide me something that brought me joy. To be honest, I felt a sense of shame that I would even require anything other than my two beautiful boys and loving husband to feel fulfilled. *Wasn't that desire ungodly? Shouldn't my family and the love of God be enough to keep me excited and overjoyed on a daily basis?* So I suffered quietly for months, afraid to bring my selfish request before God—who was already well acquainted with my thoughts and who cared so deeply about my pain.

God answered almost instantaneously, and His response moved me to tears. I sat in stunned silence; my eyes now open, staring ahead in disbelief. God had asked me to begin offering free maternity photography sessions to the women of my local crisis pregnancy center. The idea of using my new camera in such a beautiful way created such excitement within me that I right away picked up the phone and called the center's director.

The following month I began meeting with young women who were on the cusp of motherhood. I took their pictures, shared with them my excitement for the journey they were about to begin, and, I hope, gave them a real sense of Christ's love. Many of them wanted to know why I would offer this service for free, and it was my joy to reply that this opportunity was God's answer to a prayer of mine.

Taking these pictures became a ministry that brought into my life joy I could never have known was missing. Not only did the photo shoots bring joy, but they also cemented in my heart the reality of God's awareness of the details. He loves us intimately, and no desire is too small to present before Him. He answered my prayer so quickly, I'm prone to believe that He had been waiting all along for me to ask. How much time had I wasted by believing my request to serve God was selfish or vain? He delights in me and in you—and He wants to give you the desires of your heart according to His perfect will.

Daughter. Sister. Aunt. Friend. There is a reason motherhood doesn't feel like it's enough to fulfill you. We are multifaceted beings, made in the image of a multifaceted God. We were never meant to be only one thing. We are beautifully complex, capable of change, and—if we allow it—forever growing more like Christ.

The tasks of motherhood set before you may be simple, but they are anything but easy. Motherhood involves unforgivingly physical work that wrings you dry of the motivation to keep going and the energy to seek God's face about how else we can serve Him—but we must do both. We are made to be passionate co-creators with God. We are meant to not only be filled with life, but to live it to the fullest. You have always been more than a job title or a degree earned.

The tasks of motherhood
set before you may be simple,
but they are anything but easy.

Before you became a mother, you were you—completely you, uniquely you. There were hobbies and lunch dates with friends. Books you devoured in one sitting and movies you loved to watch more than once. Weekend trips to the beach and carefree laughter at silly jokes. You were and still are a beautiful, quirky, and colorful reflection of God's image. We often forget that the beauty in life's experiences exists because He, too, enjoys beauty. Perhaps you volunteered for a cause near to your heart or served in your church in some way. These things mattered to you—and to God.

Children have a way of filling up our days to the point we assume there is no time to pursue our God-given passions the way we once did. If it's not our children, we say it's our husband's fault, or even the dog's, for keeping us from reaching our true potential. If we didn't have all these messy people around to clean up after, we would be able to solve every world problem and still have dinner on the table by six, right?

It's all too easy to slip into the nagging wife role whenever your husband comes home from work—where, you imagine, he sits serenely at a desk with a hot coffee and his feet propped up, taking breaks from sitting with his coffee only to use the bathroom...alone and uninterrupted. Every day you can feel like you wage a battle at home against little dictators while your husband is living his dream—and you've given up yours to perfect mixing cheese powder into macaroni with no cheese clumps.

Do you see how easy it is for the enemy to use this to create a divide in your marriage and bitterness in your heart? This is the exact reason that you must have something for yourself that ignites passion within you. You'll simply wither without it. It's not fair or biblical to place the responsibility for our happiness squarely on the shoulders of our spouses or children. We mentally know this truth and nod our collective heads in agreement, but we also must admit that deep down we are all guilty of having this expectation on some level, or we have been at some point. Who hasn't thought to themselves, *He will never truly understand everything I do*? The truth is, he might not—but reminding him on a daily basis of his lack of awareness probably isn't moving him closer to understanding.

Ed and I have always been one another's biggest supporter of every dream we've each had for our own lives. When I went back to school to earn my credential, Ed cheered me on even though it meant my quitting a job that brought in a sizable portion of our income, and he believed steadfastly in my ability to teach even when I doubted. We all need the support of those closest to us, and though it's difficult, we must be willing to step outside of ourselves to see how we might not be providing the support our loved ones desperately need us to give them. Early on in this journey of being home full-time, I often felt both envy and guilt every morning when I heard the garage door open and Ed's car back out of our driveway.

I felt envy because I knew he was driving to a job that he was passionate about. I also felt guilty because I knew he was working so hard, and his hour-long commute meant he woke up when the sun was still hidden while I stayed in bed. If I wanted, I could (and did) wear pajama pants all day, while snacking on food I could take the time to make for myself. I knew Ed's lunches, when he took the time for them, were eaten on the run, and he often skipped them altogether to handle something that came up.

This knowledge didn't stop me, however, from snide and pointed comments when he'd get home, or from talking as though my day had been *so much worse.* Taking care of an infant is never easy, and I was exhausted after a night of little sleep, but I never once truly validated how hard Ed was working for our family—at least not in a very convincing manner. I couldn't have been fun to arrive home to. A wife, still in loungewear, looking frazzled (this is putting it kindly), complaining about how difficult her life had been all day with a baby—and completely overlooking the fact that her husband had been out all day earning the money that enabled her to be the sole caretaker of their child. (It also probably didn't help that I spent much of the time between diaper changes studying everyone else's perfect life on Facebook.)

I'm not about to suggest that you need to sugarcoat your daily life or hide your feelings from your husband or even look a certain way when he gets home. Please don't mistake what I'm about to say for some stereotypical 1950s-era homemaking advice. What I'm saying is, I'm willing to bet that, nine times out of ten, what you're complaining about in your day has more to do with you than with your spouse or your children. Those are fighting words, I know. The 2011 Jen would have rolled her eyes and maybe angry-cried at the very suggestion that she had anything to do with the way her day went. I often began my day cursing the coffeemaker for not making my coffee because I *had not yet turned it on*. I often cried while the baby cried simply out of a deep frustration I couldn't put my finger on. Exhaustion mixed with emotional depletion can be the very combination that takes you down the path to resentment and bitterness.

> *Your complaints have more to do with you*
> *than with your spouse or your children.*

I want you to hear me out, though. Don't shut this book just yet. It is vital—*vital*—that you find something for yourself that you are passionate about, you excel at, you can fit into your day, and you do just for you. You need it. Your family needs you to have it, so take the time to find it. I'm not talking about making big, grand, sweeping changes to your life. I'm talking about reigniting the flame placed in your soul by God. I'm talking about falling in love with your life again—and your role in it. The girl who loves Meg Ryan movies and dangly earrings is still in there. Find her again.

> *I'm talking about falling in love*
> *with your life again.*

This is going to take commitment on your part. By commitment, I mean that when the toddler is having a meltdown, your eight-year-old refuses to do her homework, and you have nothing left to give anyone, you still give to yourself when the dust has settled. I'm not talking about taking a bubble bath like all the magazines recommend. I'm recommending that you know and love yourself so well that you know exactly what your soul is yearning for—and then you provide it.

I clearly remember the night I decided to plunge into water I imagined was over my head. As I did every night, I lay in bed, nestled between my sleeping boys, but this particular night I held my phone above me. Their sweaty heads were pressed against my shoulders, and I tried to shield the brightness of the screen from their faces. I swiped through writing job after writing job until I found one that looked to have low enough requirements for me to apply to.

It was for a remote editing and ghostwriting position, and I would be working on the self-published work of pastors and academics across the country. Using my phone, I immediately applied, my adrenaline-fueled sweaty fingers quietly hitting the screen. It was the beginning of an inner acknowledgment that I could be more than a mother. That it was okay to want other things in addition to motherhood. It was a small step, yet it felt huge. It also felt like a tiny ray of light began to crack through the walls of the limits I had placed on myself and on my ability.

That was the very beginning of God weaving within me a dream of so much more than I could have ever dreamed on my own. The owner of the company responded the following morning—and I had the job! I was able to do the job well, and it gave me the boost I needed to go on to become a freelance contributor to *Reader's Digest*—a dream I could never have imagined for myself. A small spark ignited a full-on passion within, and I knew I was on the path I was meant for.

There is something like this for you too. Something that waits for you to discover it and, in turn, discover what dreams God has placed in your heart. Once writing became a way for me to pour back into myself again—just as it had done my entire life—I wanted to make a tangible commitment to my passion: I wanted a desk. For months I had been sitting on the couch while I wrote. It was comfortable, but my heart longed for a space that was just mine, a space where I could write articles and blogs and drink tea. I knew Ed would be completely onboard with the purchase, yet I felt a twinge of guilt at the idea of buying something just for me—and a piece of furniture at that. It felt like some kind of geeky luxury that I didn't deserve. A desk! It also felt scary. You read that right: purchasing a desk felt scary. *What if this writing thing didn't turn into anything long-term? What if buying the desk was a mistake? Where would we put the desk if I gave up writing for good?* Clearly, overthinking and over-dramatizing things is a gifting of mine that I use regularly.

As we stood in Costco in front of the perfectly sized (and priced) desk, I began to hear the little voice in my head, trying to invoke guilt. *This is money we could be spending elsewhere. Really, Jen, the couch isn't good enough? Who do you think you are?* I tried bringing up my hesitation to Ed, and he tried not to laugh at my excuses for not buying the desk.

"You need somewhere to write, and this is perfect. Let's get it," he encouraged. We all need someone to see through our own doubts and fears and push us beyond the negative voice within.

I felt so loved when we came home, and he went right to work building the desk. I decorated it with cute office supplies and found a beautiful sea glass vase to hold my pens. Once it was finished, I felt like I had taken a real step toward fulfilling an unspoken dream. I had listened to what my heart whispered, and I felt a contentment I hadn't felt in a very, very long time. If I had listened to the fearful and limiting voice in my head, I would have missed out on what God had for me. I can see now that even if I purchased the desk and gave up writing forever, it was still worth investing in myself in that way, if only for that season.

Finding What You Need

What's your desk? What thing or goal has your heart been begging for, but you've been putting off until you have the time or the resources to devote to it? As moms, we know that we are the last person we enjoy spending money on. We know it could be spent on others or on other things the entire family can use. You know what, though? Your family needs you to buy the desk or do whatever it is that will make you feel like you are working toward a dream again.

This kind of self-care is going to be different for everyone. In the next chapter we will look at how to figure out what God might be calling you to revisit—not just for you, but also for Him and His purposes. In the meantime, consider your personality type and what is fun to you. When do you feel the most fulfilled? Is it after spending time with people or after you've been by yourself with a book? If you're an extrovert and meeting up with friends for coffee is out of the question, why not spend a few minutes FaceTiming or chatting on Skype? Look for opportunities in your schedule that already exist to interact with others. Instead of heading back to the car after dropping your child off at an activity like swim practice or dance, consider hanging around for a bit and talking to the other moms. That little dose of adult interaction might be enough to hold you over until you're able to fit a larger chunk of socializing time into your schedule.

If you're more of an introvert like me, once the kids are in bed at the end of the day, spending some time reading or watching a favorite show might be just what you need to re-center yourself. For you, it might be more relaxing and soul nourishing to sit in the car or under a shady tree and read during your child's extracurricular activities rather than hang around and socialize with other moms. That's perfectly okay. You know yourself, and you have permission to give your soul what it needs.

The other thing to keep in mind is that this activity you choose doesn't have to be—and shouldn't be—something that happens only once. Speaking with your spouse about the need for time and for something of your own is so important—and I pray you have a supportive spouse who agrees with you. Maybe your husband works long hours, and it doesn't feel fair to ask him to rearrange his schedule or take on the responsibility of the kids after a long day at work. I can appreciate that.

Yet mutually supporting one another is so incredibly vital in your married life. Ed has a very demanding career, and his schedule is often filled to the brim with meetings. After we had the conversation about why I needed to take time away for myself (I cried through the conversation, naturally), he took the practical step of looking at his calendar to find an evening that he wouldn't have to work late, and then I located a Bible study that happened on that night.

I felt guilty at the time, and I can't even pinpoint exactly why I felt that way. It was a mix of guilt about handing the boys over to Ed after he had worked all day, combined with a sense of loss about missing an evening at home with all of us together. I wanted to feel fulfilled without actually having to do the thing that fulfilled me. You might feel conflicted about taking time away from your family—and you most likely will—but that feeling doesn't mean you shouldn't do it. Sometimes—most of the time—it's in the moments away, when you get a breath to yourself, that you're able to hear God, appreciate your life as-is, and refuel your tank to face the next day.

If your family's schedule allows it, try to set aside at least one evening a month to do something by yourself or with friends. Take yourself to dinner, or to a movie, or, with a coffee, to the bookstore to browse. Actually, do all of those things if you can. Go to the Bible study even if you didn't get your homework done. Go for the conversation and let the other women there pray over you and pour into you. You'll never leave empty when you go into a situation asking for God to fill you. Get to know Jesus as your best Friend who goes with you and before you into every situation. He knows you're hesitant to take this step of making time for you, that it feels unnatural and selfish. It isn't, though. Don't let the lies of the enemy keep you from becoming the person God has designed.

As I mentioned above, mutual support is key—and *mutual* means that it goes both ways. Encouraging your spouse to enjoy his own time, doing the things he most enjoys with friends or on his own, is incredibly important. It's tempting to hold on to him with a viselike grip when he's home on the weekends, I know. You've been home all week without him, braving grocery store aisles and making peanut butter sandwiches like your life depends on it, and now he wants to go out with friends? I *get it*. But even though he most likely has adult interaction at work and gets some fulfillment from it, it doesn't negate his need to have his own hobbies as well. It's a give-and-take situation—and hopefully you both understand why it's necessary for each of you.

If you don't have a very supportive spouse or if, for whatever reason, it's impossible to trade off for time away, I encourage you to find alternative ways to get the time you need to yourself. If you have relatives nearby or can locate a trustworthy sitter who will stay with your children for a few hours every week, then do it. Perhaps you have a friend who is in the same place you are, and you can arrange a day to take one another's kids so you each get a break. Time for yourself is only going to make you a more relaxed and patient version of yourself, and I'm willing to bet your kids won't mind that one bit. At the very least, take a very close look at ways you can feel like a human being again, totally separate from the all-encompassing title of Mom, a.k.a. chicken nugget-warmer-upper extraordinaire.

I believe the reason it is difficult for moms in particular to give something back to themselves is because we are tied to our children, from their very conception, in a way that only other moms can truly understand.

Some of us have been with our babies since the beginning of their existence—tied together by an actual cord that held us together as one for nine-plus months. Others of us have spent months completing paperwork and home visits just for the chance to welcome a baby into our families.

When the wait is over and our dream of motherhood is a reality, we become bonded in a way we could have never anticipated. This intimacy doesn't end after birth, as you well know. I loved breastfeeding both of my boys even after getting off to an incredibly rocky start with each (hello, scabby nipples and toe-curling latching pain). Over the years of breastfeeding, I found that it became second nature to double-check every medication or food label to see whether it was safe to consume during nursing. In fact, I had gotten so used to it that when Bradley stopped nursing, I still found myself avoiding cold medication and an extra cup of coffee. There was this moment—bittersweet, admittedly—when I realized I was no longer attached in this way with my children; what I consumed no longer affected them physically.

We mothers give to our babies unconditionally. They take what they need from us whether we are prepared to give it or not. First in their journey to our arms, then in life, and as they grow, our giving looks different. Yet throughout our children's lives, part of giving to them looks like giving to ourselves—and we are both better for it.

The Little Things Really Are the Big Things

Throughout the day it's incredibly important to pay attention to little things that will make a big difference in your attitude and the way you feel physically. There are so many ways to take care of yourself as you inch your way to beloved bedtime and also care for your kids. It can be something as simple as making yourself your favorite herbal tea when you begin to feel stressed. It might be packing the kids up in the car, buying them a cookie to keep them quiet, and taking a drive to the bookstore to research different hobbies you're interested in trying. It shouldn't be something that makes your day harder. (If strapping two or three kids in the car one more time sounds like medieval torture, then find something that doesn't require leaving the house.)

Perhaps you've always wanted to learn to knit, and now you really feel like you could knit hats for the cancer center or make Christmas gifts this year instead of buying them. Only you know what your personal interests might be—and the point is, make the time to think about them, learn about them, and ultimately do them. Recently we had the unfortunate experience of Bradley being admitted to the children's hospital for a couple of nights. Filled with anxiety and fear of the unknown, I cannot adequately express what it meant to us when a nurse brought us a blanket made by a volunteer and a stuffed bear for us to take when we left. These simple items brought incredible comfort to my little one, and I personally wanted to thank whoever was responsible for the presents. Such simple gifts of generosity are anything but simple in the hands of those desperate to receive even the smallest act of kindness.

Making time for yourself is an investment in the health and happiness of your family. It is not selfish. Once you begin regularly taking time for yourself, you will then be able to give your husband the time he needs for himself without the nagging and complaining you've been tempted to offer in exchange for his time away from home. I get it: Self-care is a foreign concept at this stage of the game. I know what it's like to dread summer because that means wearing shorts or capris—and that means taking the extra five minutes to shave your legs during showers with kids screaming outside the door.

Furthermore, finding time for yourself can seem frivolous, like a luxury you can't afford. Sometimes squeezing in a few moments for ourselves can occur in the context of time spent with our families. Right in the midst of the messy reality of life, we can make ourselves a priority while still giving our family the time with us they crave. One of our favorite things to do as a family is to take a day trip to the beach, a place where I find inexplicable solace and soul rest. On the long drive to the coast, once we've all settled into our seats and conversation has waned, I'll often listen to a podcast. Then, as my boys build sand castles and run through the sand with their dad, I love to simply close my eyes, breathe in the salt-laced air, and spend a few moments in prayer. Stealing moments to be with God and to re-center our souls doesn't require anything but a willingness to be present and aware.

We can make ourselves a priority while still giving our family the time with us they crave.

When did we buy into the lie that in order to really serve our families, we have to deny ourselves the things we once enjoyed? This lie whispers to our vulnerable hearts that good moms don't need the same things they needed before babies. Much like the enemy whispered to Eve in the garden, questioning what she really knew of God, the enemy whispers to us today, questioning our love for our children and our value to Christ. It's time to call him out on his lies. It's time to take back the knowledge of who we are to God and to stand unflinchingly on the truth that it is okay to still *need*. We may serve the needs of others every day, but we still need too.

Neediness invites a beautiful dependence on God, and without it we have no reason for a relationship with Him. Let's just admit that we desperately need Him—just as we used to—and that we ourselves still have needs that need to be met. When you take the time to do what your soul craves, you'll be the mom your children need and the wife your husband enjoys living with. Trust me on this: When you take the time to refuel, your family may notice the difference far before you do.

What does that look like for you? Every day, find something to move you toward the dream in your heart that you've hidden away for "someday." Moving toward your someday dream will do more for your present-day reality than you realize.

Here's the other thing: Be careful not to mistake a busy life for a full life. These are not the same, and your soul knows the difference. Our time on this earth is so short, so precious, that we cannot waste our days away feeling self-pity because our current season doesn't allow us to do what we think we are meant to do. There comes a point in every life when the reality of its eventual end reveals itself. Sometimes a life-changing event shifts your perspective, and other times a gradual change slowly seeps into your consciousness. For me, it was the latter. As I grow older, the limited time that I have on this planet comes more into focus, and I am aware that these days I'm living are what make up my life before I'm in front of Jesus, discussing it with Him.

*Be careful not to mistake
a busy life for a full life.*

I always told myself I would write when my boys were older. I kept putting it off until one day I realized I really felt like I was bursting at the seams, and I had to record the births of my children in writing, somewhere, somehow. So I began to write—on the notes app of my iPhone while I sat in the rocking chair and nursed my son to sleep. It felt like a safe place to start, and because I was nursing at the same time (multitasking at its finest), I was spared the familiar guilt I felt whenever I entertained the idea of doing something for myself (the horror!).

As I wrote, I felt a forgotten yet familiar surge of contentment rising within me: I felt fulfilled, as if writing was what I was meant to do. I did feel a hint of guilt creep in as I wondered if maybe I should have felt this way just rocking my baby. Was it wrong to feel such joy about something else? You already know the answer is a resounding no. Once I felt the joy of writing—that was lost along the rollercoaster of motherhood—spring back to life within me, I could no longer deny that I needed a well-rounded life to feel fulfilled.

The lopsided way I had been living, flinging every ounce of energy into my family and using the remaining fumes to brush my teeth and crawl into bed, had stolen the very spark within me that God intended me to use for His glory. We are meant to pursue those dreams God places within us. When we become mothers, we don't stop being who God created us to be. We are moms *and* women who love poetry, music, food, a sharp joke, and art. We can be all of those things still—and our families need us to be who we are and whole.

Have you uttered the very same "When the kids are older..." line? Sometimes there are things that we cannot possibly do while we have young children at home. In that case, you will have to place your dream on hold until you have more time. Other times, though, "I have to wait until the kids are older" is an excuse. It is a lie that keeps Christ's daughters firmly planted in procrastination, and we have to rise up and fight against it. Is it possible that God has something for you to do in addition to mothering your children and nurturing your family?

There are definitely seasons in life when taking on one more thing, even if it is something you want to do, feels impossible. This is okay, and you need to listen to yourself if that's where you are. (Still think about ways to be kind to yourself throughout the day, though. Make the cup of tea or use more of the good creamer in your coffee than you should. You're worth it—and the little things are actually the big things.) I am speaking the loudest to those of you in a place of monotony and boredom. Following God's call on your life doesn't mean that you have to immediately move the laundry off the couch and lead a Bible study in your home. (I can practically hear you sigh in relief.) But it certainly can be that if you want it to!

Serving God in this season of life will look different for everyone. It could be that you begin offering piano lessons or tutoring a college student each week. It might simply look like offering encouragement and positivity to others online. (There's enough negativity on the Internet to last a few lifetimes!) Ask God what He would have you do, so that you don't waste the precious breath He's given you. Your desire for joy is not at all selfish. God has a purpose for your life.

Moving toward what God has given you to do in this life might feel overwhelming at first—especially if your days are spent wiping various parts of little bodies and perfecting the skill of microwaving chicken nuggets. Overwhelming does not equal impossible, however, so it's worth putting in the effort of creating a plan—even as you work diligently to push a tiny straw through the miniscule foil circle on the juice pouch—so that you can head in the direction you feel called. (I'll never understand why sometimes those straws go in effortlessly and other times they take the concentration of a brain surgeon.)

After you've spent some time in prayer about the dreams you hold in your heart and when you feel a pull to begin moving forward with one of them, here are a few things you can do to set your plan in motion. Beginning to move in the direction God is calling you does not mean your life has to or needs to look much different than it does now. This is good news for those of you who, like me, might struggle with the idea of taking any time away from the children to focus on something for yourself—but keep in mind that this pursuit of your dream isn't just for you. This is for God, and these are the dreams He's placed within you for a reason. Our priorities must place God first, and this doesn't translate into a neglect of our children. One of the greatest gifts we can give our children is an example of what a heart devoted to Christ and His will looks like.

That said, you'll need to gather as much information as possible about what you feel called to do. At this point, you've already prayed about what you are to do, and now it is time to act. Here are my suggestions for getting started on your journey even if you don't plan to embark on it anytime soon:

RESEARCH

When I began feeling like God was leading me to begin writing in a more serious way than I had been, I spent hours online while my boys slept, researching what it took to get published—and being overwhelmed. (There were several points in time that I simply went to sleep at night letting God know that only He could make the dream of publishing a book happen, and I simply gave it up to Him.) Read all you can about your calling. Read the stories of others who have walked the path before you and study the things that led to success for them. This doesn't mean the journey will look the same for you, but it is incredibly helpful to see how things worked out for others. For me, research meant following other authors online and reading about their roads to getting published. (Spoiler alert: Many of those accounts are filled with lots of both disappointment and perseverance.)

START SMALL

I know it's tempting to rush to achieve your goal, whatever it might be, in hopes of a whirlwind of overnight success. We all want to just do it once we know what God has asked us to do. The problem with this is that oftentimes the very experiences God has planned for you will happen when you are following His call in the simplest of ways. Early in my writing journey, when I took the ghostwriting job for a small Christian editing company, I was paid nearly nothing, yet I will forever be grateful for the guidance and on-the-job education I received during that time. It was God's gracious way of allowing me to gain experience without the pressure of working for a large deadline-based company. Again, for you, this journey will look different, but the idea—start small and slowly—is the same.

What starting small looks like will depend on what you want to do. If you feel called to teach or lead a Bible study, for example, starting small might look like attending a study yourself and committing yourself to learn from the leader how to lead. It might look like finding a mentor to hold you accountable and show you what it looks like to do the thing you're feeling called to. Starting small isn't a bad thing. It means you're starting—and that's more than many people do. God tells us in the Bible to not despise small beginnings (Zechariah 4:10). The greatest things often result from the humblest start. Just taking the first step of putting a decision into action will in some way improve the way you feel about yourself and life.

TAKE AN ONLINE COURSE

The opportunities for stay-at-home mothers to pursue their dreams are greater than ever. Online courses allow you to become educated on just about anything as you sit in the comfort of your yoga pants and the couch. I once earned a second teaching credential through an online course. When Bryce was napping, I was reading and speaking with other students about online group projects. Online education may be the way you step out in faith to act now even though you're in the midst of little ones asking for another snack—and tripping over the dog for the twentieth time that day.

NETWORK

Networking is perhaps the best way to move toward your goal—but be aware that it might also move you toward it faster than you expect or want. Saying your goal out loud to others often leads to opportunities you've never imagined. Other people often have connections to those in the field or area you're hoping to join, and many times a simple phone call can place you in line to speak with exactly the person you need. God has a way of creating divine appointments for those He calls, so don't be too surprised when doors begin to open that you hadn't thought possible. I've seen this happen repeatedly in my own life, and although I know I shouldn't be surprised, God's gracious attention to my details stuns me into silence every time it happens. He is so faithful.

It is worth noting that, in this season, your purpose may solely be to serve your family at home—but this temporary assignment doesn't mean you disregard doing on a daily basis the small things that bring joy to your soul. And I guarantee, no matter where you are, there are always people you can serve right in front of you.

I was the blessed recipient of such serving on a summer morning a few years ago. On this fateful morning, Bryce was almost three and Bradley only about three months old—and I still hadn't attempted going to Target alone with both boys. Prior to this morning I would leave the boys with Ed, or I would only take Bryce with me—but I knew it was time that I got over my fear of being outnumbered and attempt to take them both. I couldn't hide at home forever—not when we needed diapers and dish soap. I pulled Bradley—still warm and sleeping from the car ride from his car seat—and placed him awkwardly in the baby carrier I wore on the front of my body. I knew he wouldn't enjoy being in the carrier for long, and the sense of urgency I felt to get Bryce from the car, get a shopping cart, and get into the store was palpable.

With Bryce walking by my side and Bradley beginning to squirm in the carrier, I walked through the doors of Target into the comforting sea of red and a blanket of cool air. I could feel Bradley's tiny knees beginning to push in defiance against my torso. Time was short. As I strolled past the dollar section and cash registers, Bryce began to whine that he wanted to ride in the cart. Ordinarily, this wouldn't be a problem, but on that day his brother hung suspended from my shoulders, and both he and I were increasingly uncomfortable. I would need to lift Bryce into the cart, while wearing Bradley and trying not to hit his head with Bryce's feet, or trigger a nonstop screaming fit (though that could have come from me instead of the baby).

I was already sweating profusely at this point, and the idea of trying to wrangle my toddler (who was quite tall for his age) into the cart was enough to make me wonder if I should just head to the deodorant aisle before making the attempt. I lifted Bryce as high as I could, got his feet onto the child seat, and encouraged him to sit.

"Put this leg here, buddy," I coaxed. He put the wrong leg in the slot. "No, buddy. This one... *This. One.*"

My pleas became more desperate as Bradley began to fuss, and sweat was surely visible through the back of my shirt. I reminded myself repeatedly that we needed diapers and that I couldn't wash my dishes without dish soap. This mission was important.

I stood there for what felt like forever, trying without success to direct my child's legs through the proper holes in the seat, when a woman and her adolescent son pulled their cart next to mine. The woman reached over, grabbed each of Bryce's legs, plunked them through the holes, and said, "There you go! I thought you could use some help!"

I nearly cried tears of gratitude when thanking her. Bradley was fully awake at this point and began to cry. I bounced him as I race-walked through the aisles, grabbing only the items I truly needed (a Target miracle), and left the store.

You may not think what that woman did was anything special, but to me she was an angel. She had been where I was in that moment, and she knew exactly how to help me. I don't know what she does or even her name, but in that moment she served someone, and it mattered. Like that woman, we can all be for one another what God calls us to be to each other: a good neighbor, day-by-day and moment-by-moment, who lives by the golden rule.

Here's the bottom line: Your children need a fulfilled mother. They need to see a light in your eyes placed there by the Light of the world. You were never meant to submit your resignation from the very things you love, the things that make you who you are in this world. The dreams you have for yourself may be on hold in this season, but that doesn't mean you can't start praying about them now or even doing small things today in preparation.

I wasn't remotely close to being a professional photographer when I offered to serve pregnant women by taking their maternity pictures, yet what I did have to offer was a blessing to them, and it sparked God-given joy in me. That photography was a solution to my joy problem that only the Lord could have offered. Let Him offer you ways to create joy in your own life and also serve Him. He cares about your details, and He will show you in breathtaking ways.

Reflection Questions

1. Have you ever asked God to give you something that was just for you? If you haven't, what has stopped you?

2. What emotions arise when you consider taking some time for yourself?

3. What can you do right now to move toward your purpose in a small way?

Talk to Him About It

Lord, I want to serve You in every way You've planned for me. Help me to know what You would have me do in this season of life to honor You. Thank You for caring about my details. I trust You, Father. Amen.

Finding Your Way Back to You

Why Your Childhood Holds
the Key to Your Joy

*There are two great days in a person's life—
the day we are born and the day we discover why.*

Anonymous

Lying on my stomach on my twin bed in 1989, I crossed my legs in the air behind me and held my pink Hello Kitty diary in front of me. It had a tiny lock and key, and I loved the idea that it was a place only I could access, a private island that only I could travel to. My thoughts, dreams, and emotions flooded through the tip of my matching pink pen as I lost myself up a stream of consciousness with no need to paddle back to shore.

Even when I was just eight years old, writing brought indescribable joy to my heart. It was more than a hobby or something

I enjoyed. It was something I needed to do to process the world around me and within me. Writing created a peace that overflowed into other areas of my life, a safe harbor in the turbulent waters of childhood that often threatened to steal my sense of calm.

We all have a God-given gift—something that we lose ourselves in whenever we do it. We feel whole, more alive, and as if we were meant to have it in our lives in some capacity. This something could be any number of things. Maybe you can still remember dancing on stage as a child, feeling as though the music captivated you in such a way it no longer felt only external, but felt like an internal beat that you moved to as well. Perhaps you felt unbridled joy when given a brand-new box of Crayolas on the first day of school, joy at the sense of limitless possibilities that the yellow box with the green stripes held. Your something may be completely unrelated to the arts. It might be a sport (though I admit—and this is probably just my endless love for Cool Ranch Doritos talking—I have a hard time imagining a sport giving me joy) or something like Pilates. Movement of the body in any form is a powerful way of connecting with the Creator.

Take a moment and reflect on your happiest memories as a child. When you were given the opportunity to engage in free play, what did you choose? When I was a little girl, nearly every time I had friends over to play, I would line them up in a mock classroom and insist that I be their teacher. (I'm sure coming to my house to play was sheer joy for them.) I'd stand in my bedroom and, while pretending that the door was an overhead screen, shine a flashlight against it and give a lecture. I loved everything about the classroom, and even when I wasn't sitting in one myself, I found a way to recreate the sense of happiness (or was it accomplishment?) I felt there. It was a surprise to absolutely no one when, as an adult, I eventually earned a teaching credential and taught third grade. Standing in front of a real classroom of my own was literally a dream come true for the little girl who made believe the Garfield dry-erase board mounted on her bedroom door was an overhead screen. In my classroom I felt as though I was exactly where I was meant to be.

These joyful moments from our childhood—perhaps appearing inconsequential in the moment—are powerful reminders of what our souls have been aching to do since the beginning of our existence. While you might not have forced your friends to pretend to be your students on a weekly basis, I'm willing to bet there's something you loved to do, or pretend to do, as a child. How can you now use that very thing to remind yourself of what God has placed within you to serve Him?

My love of teaching gave me an obvious way to serve God, but it wasn't the only way God would use me in this life. The deeper theme running through the experiences I've loved all of my life is the heart for leadership I've always possessed. I still laugh at the memory of being elected a student council member by my peers in second grade and reassuring my parents that night over dinner that I didn't vote for myself because I wanted to win fair and square. My mom smiled and said that was a noble thing of me to do—and the pride I felt was exhilarating. In many ways leadership felt natural to me—and I'm sure being the firstborn and only child for ten years had much to do with that.

What is the common theme running through each of your joyous memories? Where were you? What was the feeling that bubbled up inside of you? When was the last time in your adult life you felt something similar? As you pause to reflect, ask God to remind you of experiences in life when joy came freely to you. What were you doing? Were you alone or in a group? What was your role? Were you a leader or participant?

Don't worry about committing yourself to one thing. In different seasons of life you may be pulled in one direction more than another. Dig deeper to find what your cherished memories have in common. That theme will be different for all of us, and our responses may vary with the seasons of life. I, for instance, first followed the call to teach, gave it up, and then rediscovered my long-held passion for writing.

In fact, when I was in fourth grade, I wrote an essay about saving the environment. It was a class assignment, and I loved when I got to write in long-form for school. While the other students groaned about the three-paragraph requirement, I tried to hide my internal giddiness at the idea of being told to write an entire page about a single subject. The essays would be entered into a contest sponsored by the local irrigation district. I never thought I would win, but that didn't dampen my motivation to do the best I could. I only wanted to write.

A few months later, I stood on a stage in the front of a cafeteria packed with parents. Wearing an unfortunate (but totally typical of '80s fashion) floral dress bedazzled with large plastic jewels and puffy paint, I read my award-winning essay into a microphone over the din of whining siblings and shuffling feet. I can still recall the nervousness and barely concealed shaking of my voice as I read the words I had written. While the other parents might not have been paying attention, I found the faces of mine in the crowd.

Beaming with pride, they smiled intently back at me. They gave me the reassurance I sought and the extra courage my ten-year-old self needed to continue. Sometimes we need to remind ourselves that the loving gaze of our Father can provide us with all the encouragement we need to keep seeking His will. Our heavenly Father smiles upon us as we find the way He's planned for us to go, so let's focus on His face in the crowd rather than on those people who try to steal the attention meant only for Him.

Another thing to consider is that interests can and do change. If you can't think of anything you loved as a child that can fit in your life today as an adult, that's perfectly fine. What you found mesmerizing as a child might not be at all mesmerizing today. (When I was in fourth grade for example, I became so obsessed with learning about blue whales that I talked about them nonstop. My parents knew everything there was to know about the blue whale, bless their hearts. They swore I was going to be a marine biologist, and clearly *that* didn't happen.) What new interests have arisen for you in the past years? What are you curious about now? Take a few moments to reflect and ask God how He would have you move forward.

As I worked my way through college and established my career in marketing, my love of writing for pleasure took a backseat to writing for school and work. Some seasons of life are like that: We do what we have to just to get through, and the sacrifice is worth the greater goal.

Not until I was in my second career as a teacher did I begin a blog to record events in my life, and I knew that on a good day, I might have two readers, one of whom was my mother. The fact that few people read my words didn't matter. The joy I found in writing far outweighed any desire for my blog to become more than a space for me to write for fun.

The blog was quickly forgotten as time spent writing in the evenings after long workdays became time spent sleeping and fighting nausea in the early months of pregnancy. Thoughts of the baby I carried took precedence over writing for fun, and writing about my pregnancy felt much too personal at the time. For that season, I needed to set writing aside and focus on the emotional and spiritual journey God was taking me on as He prepared me for motherhood. Just because God has given you a passion for something does not mean He will require you to use it in every season of your life.

Listening for His gentle guidance is so important as you begin to seek His will in this area of life.

When I first decided to return to the writing I love, I fought every negative voice within that told me I wasn't qualified enough or that my words didn't matter. I saw successful authors on Instagram and Facebook doing the very thing I dreamed about, and I felt like success came only to those in other places and circumstances. *Well, their kids are older, so of course they have time to write,* I'd tell myself. *They live in beautiful areas and in homes with wraparound porches and barns converted into chic writing spaces,* I internally whined. The disappointment I felt because of my own self-talk was crushing.

You see, I had told myself a lie—and I had bought into it without knowing it. I told myself that my circumstances, my life, my smallness were simply too insignificant for God to use in any way other than caring for my children and cleaning my home. Why would He use me, with my baskets of laundry that never make it to the finish line of being put away, and my bathtubs that are always in need of scrubbing? Doesn't He want me to get things under control before He'll trust me with something bigger? Let me be the first to say, if God is waiting on me to get the laundry put away before I do something amazing, He's going to be waiting awhile. That's just the truth.

Thankfully, God isn't waiting for your housework to be perfect before He entrusts you with His holy work. His priorities are straight, and He's got people in the world waiting for the gifts only you can offer.

How important is laundry to Jesus, really? Jesus chose relationship over work: He told Martha that her sister, Mary—who chose to sit at His feet and learn instead of help with the housework—had chosen the better option. I'm going to take that as an ample dose of freedom to let my laundry sit in the baskets for one more day while I bask in God's mercy. Whether the lie of needing to have your house clean or lose the last ten pounds is keeping you from acting on the calling of your heart, I'm giving you permission to set that thing down and tell yourself the truth: None of it matters in the kingdom of God.

What lie have you told yourself without being aware of it? Regardless of what the negative voice in your head says, you have something given by God that no one else can offer the world. Many of us struggle to find a sense of purpose once we no longer work outside the home when the truth is, our purpose doesn't ever disappear or change. Our sole purpose is to know Jesus and to make Him known. That's it. It's as simple and complex as that. How we do this will look different over our lifetime, as it should when we place our focus on growing closer to Jesus and more like Him.

Maybe reading this chapter has reminded you of a joy that you've buried beneath the struggle and strain that living life brings. Does it feel selfish to consider what you lost in order to devote yourself to your family? Perhaps it's painful to reflect on what was because where you are is so far from that place of contentment. I'll let you in on a truth I learned along the way: You may have let go of the gifting God gave you for a season, but it never left you. It's still there, waiting and ready to light your eyes from within and create a renewed passion in your life.

I imagine that, at this point, you might be asking yourself how in the world you could fit in any time for something like writing, joining a choir, taking a painting class, or auditioning for a play—whatever it is that brings you deep satisfaction. What will your kids do while you pursue this passion? They'll see you pursuing your passion—that's what they'll do. I'm not going to say it's easy or that while I write my boys play peacefully for hours on end. If I said that, I might also tell you about the leprechaun who rides a unicorn through my living room every evening. It simply doesn't happen.

*What will your kids do while you pursue
this passion? They'll see you pursuing
your passion—that's what they'll do.*

What does happen is that I make time to write, and I explain (repeatedly) that I'm writing and I'll be available to play/go outside/take a walk/whatever they can think of as soon as I'm finished. I don't spend more than half an hour to an hour (and that hour is interrupted), but I give myself the time. I'm wondering if, as you read this, all those poems about babies not keeping and time passing quickly are running through your mind. Perhaps you're thinking, *If I take time for myself, I'll blink and they'll be in college. They'll look back on their lives and remember that I chose to _____ instead of spending time outside watching them blow bubbles and pick their noses!* Listen, I get it—but what if they remember that you ran hard after something that made you glow because you weren't only a mom, but also a soul on this earth meant to make a difference in more ways than motherhood? The difference you're meant to make might be within you. Don't think I'm talking on a grand scale here. I'm saying that *maybe* when you do things that make you come alive, you'll become more of the mom, the wife, and the friend you were meant to be all along.

My boys know they're loved. I spend *ample* time watching them enjoy the things that make their eyes light up—and I've learned the importance of clinging to the things that bring me joy too. I make sure my sons' needs are met, and then I meet mine. Writing makes me a better mom. It makes me a mom who is willing to give more of myself because I now have something to give.

When you meet your own needs, you are more able than ever before to meet the needs of others without resentment. Without sighing in frustration. If your kids are like mine and they had their way, you would play with them all the time. On the floor, knee-deep in Legos or Barbies, you would sit and constantly do two things: play (their way, of course) and watch (watching is a big part of motherhood, isn't it?). I'm just going to say it: I don't enjoy playing with my children as much as I think I should. I often feel guilty that sitting on the floor and playing is not something I look forward to with the zeal I wish I felt. I also have a feeling that I'm not alone in this or in other "shoulds" that attack mothers throughout the day.

While I sit on the floor, crashing monster trucks or battling Batman as I try to impersonate the Joker, my mind wanders to the dishes, the laundry, or the appointment I keep forgetting to make. I think of all the things I should be doing instead of the present activity. Herein lies the struggle, which is real. If I am doing the dishes, I feel guilty for not playing with my kids. If I am doing the laundry, I think of the bathroom that could really use a good cleaning. When I'm coloring at the table with the boys, the dishwasher is begging to be unloaded. And—you guessed it—while I'm taking care of housework, I worry that I don't play enough with my kids. I wonder internally, *Am I one of those moms who will one day look back at this season of life and regret the time lost with my kids that was spent doing the basic housework?*

When we constantly battle the attack of the "shoulds," we never find contentment in the present moment. The ability to be present in the moment—to have your mind and body exist in the same place at the same time—is gone, and a low-grade hum of anxiety takes its place. We shouldn't dare underestimate the effects this rushed way of living has on our families. Unspoken stress is contagious—and toxic—in a family. When your soul constantly feels hurried, it's more difficult to hear the whisper of God.

All of those precious little poems and graphics on social media remind us constantly that life goes by so quickly. And I agree it does. I believe, however, there needs to be a balanced narrative that speaks to reality. We need to seek out this no-frills narrative from the women who have gone before us in our churches and our families. What if we asked them about their own experiences of trying to put dinner on the table while little ones tugged on their aprons? Did they face the same internal battles about play and work that we do? Experience weighs heavier than a pretty saying every time. The older women in our lives have so much to offer us if we are willing to ask and then *listen*.

Ecclesiastes 3 tells us there is a time for everything, and I believe our lives at home echo this idea as well. Perhaps you're like me, and there is a deep sigh of peace in your body at the sight of an empty sink. When the dishes are done and the kitchen is clean, I am more relaxed and able to fully tend to the wants of my children. I don't believe we have to choose and buy into this either-or belief system that social media is trying to sell us in the form of a flowered printable. We can do what needs to be done to keep our homes functioning and ourselves content *and* be deeply invested in the lives of our loved ones.

Kids need to know that it takes work to run a household and that one of the ways we show love for others is through acts of service. I'll often tell my boys when they ask to play, "I'll play for ten minutes. After that, I need to do the dishes." They aren't exactly thrilled to have a time limit, but it sets an expectation, and when I inevitably stop playing to clean, they aren't shocked. They also know that there are plenty of other times I'll play with no time limit. Maybe this is a struggle for you too—or maybe this sounds incredibly foreign. In any event, know that once you are giving your soul what it craves by doing something that is just for you and once you are handling the housework the way you feel necessary, you will reap benefits that bubble over into your life at home with your kids.

You'll be much more willing to let the dishes sit for a little while and take the time out to give your children the joy they seek through playtime with you. You'll find an ability to be present in the moment, with less distraction, that was elusive before. Giving yourself what you need truly is the same as placing an oxygen mask on yourself before you place your children's masks on them in the cabin of a plane during an emergency. Taking care of yourself enables you to serve your children from a place of necessary fullness.

In addition to the internal benefits of living out the purpose God has planned for you, your children *need* to see you living it out. When your children see you experiencing joy using your God-given gifts, they will be inspired to find the abilities that God has uniquely gifted them with. How much easier will it be for them to find their path to fulfillment and purpose in life if they've been aware of its existence from childhood? Confidence and curiosity grow when a child knows there is a purpose for his individual life, there is a reason he was born.

I am the daughter of an artist. Growing up, I witnessed first-hand what it means to use God-given abilities to serve others and to receive joy through the work of creating. My father would spend hours poring over a piece of art, sketching and researching, for the sole purpose of creating something beautiful. Working a full-time job, he created the art of scrimshaw in the moments he could set aside in the evenings and on weekends. His example taught me that our gifts and abilities are still worthy of our time even if they are not how we make our living. My dad also taught me to focus on the value a God-given gift has for my soul even if that skill never earns external approval. My father's scrimshaw was, in fact, featured in galleries up and down the coast of California, yet he never placed an emphasis on the admiration his work received. Instead, scrimshaw was something he created with God, and that was enough.

The value of pursuing our own God-given gifts is clearly communicated to our children even if we cannot see it in the moment. Pursuing your own gifts might not produce something tangible like a piece of art. Although we are all creative—because we are made in the image of the Creator—the demonstration of your gifts and abilities will most likely look different from those of the people around you. It's also possible that your calling isn't to create, but to solve, assist, or cure. Perhaps you love all things science or technology related, and you find joy in researching trends and advances. Maybe you find profound joy in organization, and you miss the order of a well-organized office. Why not stay aware of the latest developments in your field so that you're up to speed upon your return to work if—*when*—that day comes? What if your love of organization could be the start of a business helping others to live in less cluttered homes? It may be that God's purpose for you will be found in the pursuing of a dream you were already walking toward.

My earliest memories, specifically of my mother lying next to me in bed, are of her telling me stories she imagined and then spoke aloud. A few of them became my favorites and to this day are ingrained in my mind as if she told them yesterday. Recently, she typed one out for my boys to have, and the details were still etched in her mind as well. Her gift of imagination nourished my own early sense of creativity.

Our children will see the fulfillment that is naturally born within us when we follow God's purpose and will for our lives, and they will come to understand that they, too, have purpose in this life. They can also see that external praise is never as fulfilling as the feeling of walking with God, and they will learn to look to Him alone for direction and approval. What does your life say about who God is? Even when we don't say a word, our lives communicate His power and involvement. Christ told us this life would be difficult, but does yours speak of the victory and triumph we can still claim in Him?

With God, the ultimate Creator, leading us, we can follow on the path He has prepared for us with excitement and anticipation of what He has in store. He Himself found happiness in His creation, pronouncing it "good" after the world and its inhabitants were complete. The Bible instructs us to delight in the Lord, for He will give us the desires of our heart (Psalm 37:4). God has placed the desires in our heart for a purpose. There's a reason that you long to learn more about the orphan crisis or you dream of starting your own business. These are the very things that make you unique, and they are to be used in a specific way in the kingdom of God.

When we first become mothers, creating something in addition to the child we just birthed feels unnecessary. We created a human. This feels like the place where we drop the mic. We have done enough. I imagine that, after going through the lengthy and grueling process of paperwork, home visits, and helping their child adjust to a new life, mothers who adopted children also feel they're more than justified in setting their own interests or gifts on a shelf. The truth is, in certain seasons of life, you are justified in saying, "No more. Not. One. More. Thing."

After the births of both of my boys, I rejected the idea that I should attempt to be creative. I created meals (chicken nuggets for my older son and breast milk for my younger), and games to play, and a schedule for our days with clearly outlined naptimes (Can I get an amen?), and that felt like enough creating. My brain and body were exhausted, and I needed a drip line of coffee. Using God-given gifts outside of raising my tiny children felt overwhelming, and—if I'm being honest—neglectful, selfish, and foolish.

Perhaps this is the place you find yourself: You want to find a way to nourish your soul in a creative or joyful way, and it feels impossible. You feel as though you have nothing else to offer the world or even your family. You need to know that feeding your soul is possible and that you do have so much to offer. When we stop doing whatever makes our soul sing, the void that results becomes evident to all who know us. The sparkle in our eyes dims a bit. We seem less motivated and less like ourselves.

Feeling this void doesn't mean that your children are any less important to you or loved by you. We are not limitless; only God is. In fact, when you make an intentional effort to find fulfillment by co-creating with God, however that might look, you are investing in your children's mother. A fulfilled, whole, and joyous mother is far more effective than one who feels worn down, martyred, and as though her life's purpose consists of an endless search for a non-leaking sippy cup. We are meant to keep creating long after we procreate or adopt.

Why Not You?

On a Saturday morning a few months ago, I was on my way to the grocery store, my weekly routine in full swing. I was listening to another author's podcast and feeling increasingly defeated about the possibility that I would one day be able to publish the book you are now reading. I sat at the stoplight, awaiting the green arrow to turn, when a single thought popped into my head unexpectedly: "Why *not* you?" I sat with the thought for a moment, and the confidence in God's ability to do the impossible began rising in my chest. By the time I reached the grocery store, I was full of hope and picking out produce with a joy that I'm sure most of the other shoppers found annoying and possibly disconcerting. I knew—deep within and without question—that God can do anything.

In that moment, I realized that every single person who has

ever done anything they dreamed of had sat where I sat, living a normal life, tempted to believe the lie that our God is small. This lie had silently woven itself into my thought process, and I wasn't aware it existed until it was called out in that moment I waited for a light to change. The truth is, when you follow the leading of the one true God, He will make a way. He is able. He will swing open doors and knock down obstacles because you are following Him, not the world. The world will always offer us discouragement, but Jesus offers us what the world never can: His hope, His power, and His ability. All things are possible through Him. Your dreams may feel far-fetched—but have you ever wondered why you have those dreams to begin with? Who placed those dreams in your heart? They are there for a reason—to show God's glory, through you, to a world in desperate need of the hope of Jesus.

In this season of your life, moving toward the purpose God has placed on your heart might be the simple act of reading about it when you have a free moment to spare. Maybe this moment comes as you sit on a park bench while your kids play on the playground and in between their requests for snacks and water. Or maybe you listen to audible books or podcasts about your dream while you do laundry or wash dishes. I've learned so much by listening to podcasts while unloading the dishwasher. If you look hard enough, there is always room in your day to grow closer to God and nearer your calling.

As a writer, I rarely have large chunks of time during the week that I can spend crafting an article or a blog post. Most of my writing is squeezed into 15- to 30-minute chunks spread throughout my day, in between morning devotional times, homeschooling, meal times, and running errands. I've also been very purposeful in creating a routine for my children and myself that provides ample space to just be. Neither of my boys is in more than one sport at a time, if any, and with them both being so young, Ed and I don't place great value on sports at this point. As they grow, we will reassess what is important to our family and what is worth being placed into our daily schedule. A busy life is not the same as a fulfilled life, and it is vital that we remember this truth when creating a schedule for our children and ourselves.

Owning the Benefits of Being Home

There are certain benefits of being a stay-at-home mother that we cannot argue with. Next to sleeping in every day and binge-watching Netflix (sarcasm font), this is one of them: We have the unique ability to schedule our time in a way that supports our own fulfillment and that of our children. I'll forever be grateful for the mundane but beautiful consistency I've been able to create in our daily schedule. There's a simple beauty that's born out of living life without the rush of the outside world.

I've never been forced to wake my boys according to a work schedule or to hurry them through breakfast while combing their hair. In stark contrast, our lives are slow and gentle. Our mornings are filled with sleepy cuddles before we head downstairs for breakfast. Every kiss pressed against a little cheek—still warm and pink from sleep, indented with pillow lines—reminds me of the extravagant gift of being home with my babies. I would never trade these priceless gifts scattered throughout my day.

Such moments in life of being home with our children remind us, in a deep and instinctual way, we've been called to be moms. In the same way that I knew exactly the way to hold my babies and soothe them, I knew that returning to work felt deeply unsettling to my soul. It's important to make note of what feels good and right as well as what feels the opposite and to trust the still, small voice within. We can trust ourselves because we are not alone. The Holy Spirit lives within. Our Helper and Counselor, He guides us in the way we should walk.

And I've realized on my walk that being home with my children for these simple moments will always outweigh any love or devotion I had to my career. There's no contest. I have profound peace about my decision to be home even though I wrestled with it fiercely. This peace, however, doesn't by any means negate the emotional aspect of the loss of a career. Remember, we can hold both sorrow and joy in the same heart, at the same time. God has made us beautifully complex in this way.

The blessing of slow and intentional living is unique to stay-at-home motherhood and one that we must steward well. The gift of time and the ability to determine how we spend it is a gift we cannot take lightly—nor should we let these precious hours in our days slip by without notice. Find the time to explore what makes your heart beat wildly. Explore with focus and purpose the interests of your children. What makes their eyes shine a bit brighter, and what do they talk about endlessly? You have been given this gift of slow, purposeful parenting, and when you use it to deepen the bonds between you and your children, you are using this gift well.

Even with a schedule free of obligations, though, the day can easily be eaten away by life. We've all had the kind of day when drinks are spilled on carpet, jars of salsa shatter across the tile floor, and, when suddenly the dog seems lethargic, an unplanned visit to the vet is in order. (Maybe this is just me? For your sake I hope so!) If you still feel like finding your gift to be used for God is one more stressor in an already stressed-out life, I again encourage you to go straight to Him and ask what He would have you do to express His glory and love to people. He is so faithful to give direction when His servants humbly ask how to serve and are willing to follow His leading. When we purposefully use our given breaths on earth to glorify God and show gratitude for His gifts, we make much of our time here. We create for our children and ourselves a life well spent, a life that shows the world who Jesus is. What's better than that?

Reflection Questions

1. What is the common thread that runs through your joyous childhood experiences?

2. In what context have you believed the lie of a small God in your life? What feels too big for Him?

3. What activity can you put into practice right now to begin nourishing your soul daily?

Talk to Him About It

Thank You, Father, for the gift of joy in my life. Thank You for bringing to mind the moments in my life when I felt free and joyful. Help me, Lord, to know how I can return to that place now, as a mother. Speak to me and I will listen; please open my heart to hear You, Father. I trust You. Amen.

Making Friends with Telemarketers

Fighting the Battle of Loneliness

Our language has wisely sensed these two sides of man's being alone. It has created the word "loneliness" to express the pain of being alone. And it has created the word "solitude" to express the glory of being alone.

Paul Tillich[4]

It's so easy," I told the cashier at the supermarket as she rang up my groceries. I was giving her my recipe for cake balls, providing her with step-by-step directions whether she wanted them or not. She seemed so excited to make them, and I thought to myself that she seemed like someone I would love to hang out with. She had an awesome sense of humor that leaned toward sarcasm, and I imagined that we'd become BFFs in no time.

I decided to go for it. "Here's my number, you know, if you run into any problems when you make them," I said as I wrote my name and cell phone number on a crumpled receipt I grabbed out of the many in my purse. She smiled, hesitated a brief second, and thanked me. This was a one-sided attempt at friendship. I paid for my groceries and sprinted to my car, the reality beginning to hit that she was simply being nice. She wasn't desperate for friendship in the way I had been since becoming a stay-at-home mom.

The truth was, she was surrounded by coworkers-turned-friends at her job, just as I had been. She wasn't longing for adult interaction on a daily basis or looking for ways to make one day look different from the last. Of course, these were all assumptions I made, and I may have been completely wrong. All I knew was that I longed for interaction with someone older than four, someone who wouldn't scream if I hadn't dried all the residual water drops from the outside of the Playtex sippy cup. Was that too much to ask?

I returned home that day feeling embarrassed by my own desperation. *Was I really so pathetic I just tried—and failed—to set up a mom-date at the grocery store?* I continued to feel shame about that interaction for a long while. For much longer than it takes to actually make cake balls—which, at least for me, is a long time. I never expected that staying home would make me so awkward in social situations. I used to thrive on small talk!

When I made the decision to stay home with Bryce, I naively assumed I would only be giving up a job that I loved, a place I went every day, but not much more. What I actually gave up was an entire life filled with relationships that I had built over time. All of those moments spent chatting at the copy machine in the teachers' lounge, the daily lunches spent moaning about less-than-stellar class test scores, the inside jokes shared during meetings or recess—those things mattered to me. Those things gave me a sense of comfort, of belonging, and of worth.

A few times, for a day here and there, I returned to teaching as a substitute only to find that it's true that you can't go home again. I would arrive at a different school site than the one I had taught at and sit in the teachers' lounge during lunch while the other teachers shared the camaraderie that I missed so much. To them, I was an unknown substitute, and I so desperately wanted to tell them that I had actually been one of them just a year or two before. The students I taught did not know me or have a relationship with me. I was foreign to them as well. I missed the comfort of a classroom that felt like home. With substitute teaching only adding to the mixed emotions I felt about resigning, I knew I needed to take a break until more healing had taken place.

When you lose your work community, you're not only missing out on daily interaction with peers, but on celebrations as well. Because I was still connected with so many of my former colleagues on social media, I had a front-row seat to every Christmas party, baby shower, wedding, and get-together that I was no longer a part of. Every picture of my friends together—joyful and celebrating without me—felt like a personal jab. Even though I knew it was absurd to feel intentionally excluded, those Facebook postings only added to the loneliness and isolation I felt within the four walls of my home.

It's worth noting that our own mothers and other women who have walked this road ahead of us did not have the thorn of social media in their sides, those constant reminders of what continued on after they walked away from jobs for the sake of their children. It's an act of self-care to know your own limits regarding social media and to distance yourself from it while you process your emotions. I repeatedly reminded myself that there were downsides to my career as well and that there were more perks to being home with my babies than there would ever be if I continued working outside the home.

This sense of loss revealed to me how important a sense of community can be in all of our lives, but even more important is being in communion with the only One who matters. When our identity is firmly established as a child and servant of the Savior, the personal losses no longer carry the same sting they once did.

Loneliness takes many forms and is often the result of a different set of circumstances for all of us. For me, I felt as though the isolation experienced during that time was inevitable. I couldn't relate to many in my peer group of other stay-at-home moms simply because they weren't exactly like me.

At the park I met other moms with young children, and the conversation would inevitably turn to the best local preschool programs. I had done extensive research of my own, and coupled with the intimate knowledge of my son, I knew I wouldn't be placing him in a program. When the other moms heard this, they often withdrew just enough for me to know I had either hit a nerve or made them doubt their own decision, and I never knew what to say or do in response. My choice to keep Bryce home during his early years was simply my own, based on what was best for our family, but I left those park outings with the distinct feeling that it would be impossible to find true community among other mothers.

Desperate to find my people, I joined a local mom's group that prided itself on its goal of providing women with a sense of belonging and community. I hoped that the group would provide the adult interaction during the day that I lacked. Upon my first meeting, a playdate at one of the members' extravagant homes, I knew I was not likely to find community here. The women— most of them the wives of prominent businessmen in our small town—were confused when I mentioned that I missed the joy I found in my career.

"Why would you ever work if you didn't have to?" asked the hostess of the playdate while wiping down the granite countertop in her extensively upgraded kitchen. The other mothers nodded in agreement. Her question left me feeling awkward, as though we came from entirely different worlds. I pondered whether I was crazy to miss my career as she told the other mothers about her Hawaiian vacation plans, pausing only to put her daughter in the nanny's car to be shuttled to a ballet lesson. All of the mothers in this group seemed welcoming and kind, yet I couldn't shake the feeling that it was not meant for me to be a regular part of the group.

Adult Friendship Is Hard

Several times during this period I ran into former colleagues and supervisors. The conversations that ensued were always enjoyable, but when the perfunctory question "So what are you up to?" was asked, I never knew how to respond without sounding like my life was empty of any meaningful activity. Responding with "Laundry, dishes, and keeping the children alive" never felt right, so I always settled with the "Oh, you know, just life," response. As if the act of mothering could never compete with being a mom *and* having a job outside the home, I allowed my insecurities to drown the value of the important work I was doing.

Perhaps you, too, have tried and failed to force a sense of community in your own life. It's humbling, isn't it? Those first awkward attempts to birth new friendships can have labor pains of their own, and it's tempting to give up. I left such interactions feeling confirmation of what I suspected: I fit nowhere. The stay-at-home mothers were quite content to be home, and the working mothers were either envious of me or pitied my simple life. None of these assumptions were accurate, but in my search for my identity, they seemed completely plausible.

Staying home with small children every day is isolating and lonely—I don't have to tell you that. The endless cycle of housework, meal prep, playtimes, nap times, and bedtimes would make even the most self-assured person begin to question where friendship or community could even fit into the schedule.

I know it's tempting to search for a group of women to belong to and then get frustrated when it doesn't work out. We tell ourselves that everyone else has what we want—and the social media pictures of groups of women away on "girls weekends" laughing on the beach only serve as a depressing reminder of what we don't have. It's undeniable that some people have a tightknit group of girlfriends who have been friends for years. It's also undeniable that, for the rest of us, this just isn't our reality.

If you have a group of friends that has survived the test of time, be grateful for the blessing of amazing friendships and enjoy them. What a gift you've been given! For those of us who fall into the "Still Searching" category, hear this: I don't believe we are all made for large groups of deep friendships. We are all made for community, but I absolutely believe this can be found in one or two other women with whom we can be our authentic, flawed, and beautiful selves. Over the last several years, I have had to confront my own belief of the lie that every other woman has a large group of best girlfriends who randomly stop by for coffee, share clothes, and hang out to chat at all hours of the day. The enemy loves to lie to us—especially about topics that reside in the softest places in our hearts. Honing the ability to recognize truth is one of the most valuable skills we can possess. Recognizing Satan's lies can, in fact, be the difference between spiritual life and death.

My best girlfriends live hours away, and I'm so thankful for technology. Texts and calls can do so much to squelch feelings of isolation. I've come to realize that although I crave the types of friends who can stop by any time of day, those would also be a source of stress because I need a schedule—and advance notice so I can clear the living room of toys, empty string cheese wrappers, and juice boxes. The truth is, I like to plan, and the spontaneous visit from a friend might leave me more stressed out than relaxed. For better or worse, this is my personality, and it is something I want to work on.

Adult friendships can be complicated especially once kids are added to the mix. Parenting styles vary wildly from one family to the next, and the differences can be enough to drive a wedge in what was a strong friendship. As you navigate finding new friends in this season of life, know that disappointment is often a part of it. Not all new friendships will stand the test of time—and that's okay. I believe God often brings women into our lives when we need them most. They teach us what we need to learn in that season, and we grow. It can be hurtful when such a friendship comes to an end or when you simply drift apart, but know that the time you invested was still worth the effort. Sometimes we learn more from the end of something than the beginning, and friendships are no exception.

Another note about friendship. Don't underestimate the importance of your relationship with your husband in this season of life. Sometimes I wonder if God has allowed my friendships with women to move to the periphery so that the relationship with my husband can take its rightful place in my life. When we look to our other half to be a true partner, soul mate, and the best friend he's promised to be, our marriages thrive in a way I'm not sure they can otherwise. We've made a vow to our husbands to choose them over and over until death do us part, and there's no one else who we've promised the same.

The truth is, even if a magical best friend appeared at your door-step tomorrow with glazed donuts and coffee (if we're imagining perfect friends here, she will also have the *Pride and Prejudice* PBS miniseries with Colin Firth under her arm), the man you've pledged to be with forever should still be the one you confide in first and foremost. Truth be told, however, there will always be things only another woman can understand. (I learned this quickly when trying to explain to Ed the purpose of a menstrual cup. I'll never forget the horror that ran across his face while he tried to remain understanding.)

Our relationships with women are integral in our lives. We need them for so many reasons, not the least of which is the simple knowledge that we aren't alone in our struggles. We need girlfriends for mentorship, nursing cream recommendations, and to slow the tears of exhaustion that only another mother understands. We need each other, plain and simple. Finding such friendships is difficult, I know. Like everything else in life, though, if God isn't in it, we shouldn't want it. God will often prune our lives of the very things that hinder our growth, and though it feels painful at the time, we must desire His best for our lives, and no less.

When the Past Isn't Pretty

A few months ago I was sorting through old e-mails when one e-mail to a friend from years ago caught my attention. I opened the e-mail expecting to see old inside jokes and some reminders of the past I had long forgotten. Instead, as I read the words I wrote to her, my face began to burn, shame searing its way into my heart. My words to her were about another friend of ours, and I wasn't kind. I was snarky, clearly envious of this friend—and it wasn't pretty. I sat in silence, barely recognizing who I used to be—enough so that I double-checked that I had indeed sent it.

You see, before I made this journey into motherhood, I was known among close friends for my snark and sarcasm. I was often the one who made others laugh at a celebrity's expense and, apparently via e-mail, even at the expense of those I called friends. I read gossip magazines and watched reality shows—oblivious to the impact they had on my mind and my view of others. I often turned my cutting wit toward myself and offered copious amounts of self-deprecation—anything for a laugh.

After I read this e-mail that was an unexpected and ugly window into my past self, I sat in the shame it produced, but the realization that this wasn't who I was anymore began to nudge its way into my soul. I would never write such an e-mail now. The Holy Spirit within me would offer a correction long before I hit "send." Sometimes an unobstructed view of the past is the only thing that clearly reveals the truth of the present.

I was a Christian when I wrote that note, but clearly Jesus had a lot of work to do within my heart. Although I had the Holy Spirit to convict me about my behavior, I simply wasn't listening. I wanted the approval (and laughter) of man far more than I wanted to hear and obey His voice of correction. Maybe you've been there, in a circle of friends who love hearing your latest joke or gossip. It feels good in the moment, doesn't it? That kind of approval from others is addicting, and it's a seductive way the enemy draws us further from Jesus, often without us even noticing. It's one reason that social media can be a slippery slope into a self-absorbed world. I post inspirational stories and try to point others to Christ with it—but I have to call myself out when I'm monitoring the response of others to a post more than I'm paying attention to my connection with God.

Not until all of the friends, the magazines, and the reality shows were stripped from my life was I able to slowly grow to be more like Jesus. My life was being pruned, and what fed my mind was being changed. The process was so slow I was entirely unaware it was happening.

I no longer had an opportunity to gossip in the teachers' lounge or to try to tell the best jokes at staff parties. It was, quite literally, Jesus and me. Day in, day out. A breaking down, a remolding, a rebuilding of a life into His likeness. He loved me too much to allow the hollow shell of who I thought I was to be the final word. He had something else in mind for this girl and His glory. Who we are when we are alone with God is who we truly are.

> *Who we are when we are alone*
> *with God is who we truly are.*

Maybe you've had this experience yourself, and instead of reality shows and magazines, you've been stripped of an addiction to online shopping or even a nightly glass of wine that turns into three. What are you dependent on instead of God? Anything that keeps us from walking in step with the Lord is nothing that we want. Let it be pruned—and bless the One who holds the pruning shears. May we want only Him.

God allowed some relationships and superficial interests to drift out of my life for a reason: so that I could grow into who He wants me to be, so that I can be more like Jesus. The loss was painful, and to be honest, I still miss some of these friends, but I simply couldn't grow in Christ while they remained so intimately connected to me. Jesus knows what we need to reflect His image while in this skin. His goal isn't that we lose those we love, but if their presence in our life is a stumbling block to our relationship with Him, He's going to move it.

Sometimes the people we hold the closest are also those who stifle the work of Christ within us. They may or may not be Christians themselves, but it's more important to evaluate who we are when we are with them rather than who they are. After time with them, do you hear the whisper of the Holy Spirit reminding you not to gossip or judge? Is there a sliver of guilt and shame in your heart after you utter words that slipped out so easily that you surprised yourself?

Rather than beat yourself up, take a moment to consider what you and your friend are bonding over. If your relationship is more about who you can tear down rather than how you can build each other up, it's time to evaluate the place of this friendship in your life. Our friends are on their own paths and will one day meet God, but we are only responsible for our own journey. I cringe when I think about the ways I've damaged the witness of Christ during my past days of prompting laughter at any cost. I can only pray He will use it for His glory somehow, and as Paul said, I will continue to take off the old creation and put on the new, in Christ.

We are only responsible for our own journey.

God doesn't want us to be lonely and bitter. He wants us to remain close to Him and close to others. He designed us for relationship, first and foremost, with Him. If we aren't tending to our relationship with Him, we throw every other relationship off balance. It's all too easy for our focus to veer from serving God and others to serving ourselves. Spending time reading the Bible, meditating on God's blessings, and reflecting on His responses to past hurts and the times He proved His presence are excellent ways to move into a posture of humility and a nearness to the Father. We can be honest with God during prayer. Our heartfelt requests and our raw pain do not surprise or offend Him.

My younger son, Bradley, is three, and his gentle spirit is often perplexed by the harshness of this world, especially when an interaction with his brother hurts his feelings. He runs to my arms in tears and throws his pudgy arms around my shoulders. He will tell me in great detail about every action or word that hurt his feelings—and I cherish the opportunity to mend his broken little heart with love and warmth that only a mama can offer. My words of tenderness and encouragement never fail to slow and eventually halt his tears.

And so it is with our heavenly Father. He longs to hold us as we process difficult emotions, including anger, bitterness, or sadness. Our God is big enough to handle whatever we send His way. When we run to His arms in tears, we can be assured that He cherishes the chance to soothe us with His love, His Word, and His comfort.

What a New Puppy Reminded Me About God

We recently welcomed into our family a shih tzu puppy we named Bailey. He's four pounds of fluffy defiance that never fails to keep me on my toes. He loves to eat—but only the things he's not supposed to. Toilet paper, wood, worms—you name it, Bailey will eat it. We've got the $200 X-rays to show for it. A few weeks ago he was playing in the backyard when a piece of tree bark looked mighty appetizing. He grabbed the chunk of wood and ran behind one of our most prickly bushes. He's stubborn, and he's smart.

At first, as he continued chomping, I tried to get to him from the edges of the bush. It was no use. I knew the only way to get to him was to go through the center of this tree I wish we had never planted—and I knew I'd be poked and scraped in the process. I was able to get to Bailey this way—I have the scraped arms to prove it—and get the wood out of his mouth. *What I won't do for this dog*, I thought. It was then that I realized that Jesus does the same—and has done the same—for us. He comes for us in the hard-to-reach places—the ones that ensure His pain—with no hesitation. He was pierced for our sins, and by His stripes, we are healed. What He won't do for *us*, sisters. *What He won't do for us.*

I often find myself feeling a desperate need for my boys to know the depth of my love for them. I smother them with kisses and hugs any chance I get, pepper *I love you* throughout the day, and display a genuine interest in the things they enjoy. I want them to know this love that threatens to burst the seams of my heart. The love that destroyed my previous definition of it in the best of ways and rebirthed it with a richness I could have never foreseen. My love for my children is immeasurable and eternal, and I'm guessing you feel the same for your children. I can't help but think that this must have been how God feels about us, so He sent us Jesus. With a desire for us to know the vastness of His unlimited love, God gave us the ultimate gift: the reconciliation to Him we never deserved, a relationship and a friendship with the God of the universe. He is the Author of friendship.

When we seek God first and share with Him our desire to be in community with at least one other woman who can relate to our life struggles and joy, He will hear. His ways are not our ways, and a woman with the same passion for *Friends* trivia and singing along to Disney Junior show theme songs might not ever appear on your doorstep (this is probably a good thing), but He is faithful to hear your heart and provide you with His best plan for your life. You always win with Jesus. You are always covered in His grace and love. Always.

I know it's tempting to sit at home, give up on interacting with others, and wallow in the lack of adult conversation. It makes no sense at all that we would bemoan being lonely yet lack the motivation to reach out to others—but it's what we do. I have a feeling that's exactly the enemy's plan. Isolation leads to loneliness and a belief that our efforts will be fruitless. It's there, in the quiet of our own need for connection, that we most need to turn to God's Word for a reality check. We cannot allow the enemy to win this battle in our minds. God says in Matthew 18:20 that where two or more are gathered, there He is. Why would this be included in His Word if it were not to be an encouragement to be among others? The enemy will fight to keep us isolated not only to squelch our connection with others, but also to try to keep us from closeness with God.

It's hard to find the motivation to leave home, especially for those of us whose children are not yet school age or who have chosen to homeschool. We have no real reason to leave the house except for the fact that we aren't called to be hermits. I—as much as the next person—love cozy days spent at home curled up with a jar of Nutella, but when this becomes a habit and it's all you do, it might be...No, it definitely *is* time for you to get out of the house and talk to adults.

Jesus chose twelve disciples, and none of them were who we would expect the Savior of the world to choose as a friend. But He wasn't looking for people just like Him—no one could ever meet that requirement anyway! When we give ourselves the freedom to love others in the way Jesus commands, we open the door wider for friendships we could never anticipate.

We worry less about what we are getting from friends, and we focus more on what we can give to others as Jesus works through us in practical ways. A deep and lasting friendship won't just appear at your door, but it might begin with an offer of childcare for a mom's older child while she takes her baby for a well-check or with giving your child's teammate a ride home from soccer practice so her mom doesn't have to miss an important meeting. We can be the friends we wish we had even when it feels awkward or new. How many new friends have we never made simply because we thought, *She's going to think I'm so weird/desperate/presumptuous*?

Our communities will look different from the way they used to, but do we really want them to look the same as we grow into a closer likeness to Christ? Sometimes change is the outward evidence of internal growth. When Christ is our focus, our intense desperation to find friends will often fade because He truly is enough for all of us. Still, it is worth the effort to continue to reach out and pray for a friend or two to come your way.

If you've tried mom groups and park playdates and you're still coming up empty on the friend front, it just might be time to switch up your methodology a little. You're not alone in your desire to stop telling the guy selling solar panels your life story when he calls, and there's a community out there with a "you"-shaped hole that is awaiting your arrival.

Finding a group of women you feel comfortable with might mean that you seek out groups based on things other than motherhood. Looking outside of the mom category and into things like Bible studies and hobby-based groups will most likely put you in contact with other moms without putting the emphasis on that part of your life. Let's be honest, it's really nice to leave our mom title at home for a bit and go into the world as just us—no diaper bag, no snacks, and no water bottles bulging in our purses.

A few summers ago I joined a women's Bible study that met

close to my home on Monday nights. Originally the meeting place was far across town, and I was tempted to stop attending after the first night. I felt so guilty, waving goodbye to the boys and Ed as soon as he came home from work. It didn't help that there was no one I knew in the group, and the loud Panera we met in only added to my anxiety.

"I don't think I'm going to go back," I told Ed when I got home that first night. "I don't think it's my type of Bible study."

Ed tried to reason with me. "You never feel comfortable with things like this at first."

He was right, of course, but I wasn't going to admit that. I was too stubborn and emotional to be clearheaded. I wanted instant friendships, and I wanted to instantly feel safe and comfortable with the group of women. Did these look like women I could someday take a beach trip with? None of them wore a sun hat or laughed constantly like the images I saw on Facebook! Clearly they were not my tribe.

A few days after the first meeting, I received an e-mail from the study leader, saying the location had been changed. The Bible study was now being held one street over from my home. I knew in my heart that this was God meeting me where I was (quite literally) and providing for me in a way that only He could know I needed Him to. Now, since my commute was less than three minutes long, I was able to stay and chat a bit with Ed before leaving each week, and I would return home to my boys before bedtime.

Every Monday I looked forward to peeling off my yoga pants, throwing on a pair of capris and a cute top, and leaving my favorite boys in the world to go meet with other women of all ages. In a more intimate setting, I was able to see that the women in the group were kind, welcoming, and had a great sense of humor. All the women in the group were moms, some much further along the path than

I was, and their sage advice and calm assurance were comforting. Others in the group had little ones the same age as mine, and we were able to touch on some of our shared struggles without spending too much time wallowing in our parenting woes.

When I was able to strip away the self-imposed pressure of seeing each woman as a potential best friend whom I would someday vacation with, I was able to focus on Christ and seeking Him. Our goal was to grow into a deeper relationship with Jesus, and these Bible study women couldn't have cared less if I breast- or bottle-fed my boys or about the fact that we chose to co-sleep. They called me by my name, never whined that the last fruit snacks were eaten, and allowed me to complete a sentence. It was just the breath of fresh air I needed at a time when motherhood threatened to swallow me whole.

Although social media has its share of negatives, it can also be a place to find friends on those days you just can't muster the strength to get everyone's shoes on and head out the door. During my first pregnancy I joined an online community of women who were all—like me—expecting babies in September of that year. There are over one hundred of us, spanning the nation, and our friendships have continued long past the births of our babies. For six years we have seen one another through the valleys and peaks of motherhood, including the loss of precious babies, serious childhood illnesses, and the loss of our own parents as well. These women are more than Internet profiles in my life; they are an endless source of support and laughter. I'm so grateful for the way God has gifted me with a community that might seem untraditional, but is nonetheless real and life-giving.

All of this is to say, we can't ignore the possibility of finding friendship and community with people who don't share our own zip code. Yes, real-life friends (as opposed to virtual friends) are valuable and important to seek, but let's not forget that friendships that are just as meaningful and important can exist through many channels. We cannot pretend to know what God's plan for community will look like in our lives. He uses all things to bring glory to Himself and goodness to His children.

I'll be the first to admit, however, that sometimes I still struggle with the loneliness of being home. As a writer, I do much of my work alone with cartoons and yelling children providing background noise. It's easy for me to be so consumed with my work that I forget to give myself what my soul is craving. I have this habit of imagining what life will look like in the future, and it's always so much better than life is now. I flash forward twenty years, and I create this serene picture in my mind of what I'll be doing. I'm sure this sounds incredibly simple to most (dream bigger, Jen!), but I see myself sitting alone at my kitchen table. Music is playing softly, I have a fresh cup of coffee, and my Bible is open in front of me. I'm studying God's Word in a quiet home, and I have as much time as my heart desires to do so.

It occurred to me about a month ago that if I made a simple change in my morning routine, I could, for the most part, make my future dream a present reality. So now I take my Bible and coffee to the kitchen table instead of the living room couch. Sure, it isn't quiet by any means, but it feels different. Once I moved where I sat to meet with God in the mornings, I felt more peaceful, and I felt like I had really met some kind of goal I had for myself. I still giggle at the simplicity of it all, yet I think there's something there to dig a bit deeper for. I don't have music playing softly in the background, and I certainly don't have all the time I desire to study as deeply as I'd like, but doing what I can in the present moment feels so much more satisfying than continuing to dream about a future that I doubt will be free of challenges. Chances are, my future self will find the quiet of the kitchen deafening, and I'll desperately long for the sound of cartoons and shrieking children (or not, but let's just say that I will). The point is, if there is something we can do now to shift our perspective on our current season of life, why not do it?

After I adjusted my morning routine and made the life-altering change of moving to the kitchen, I looked at other things in my life that I had unconsciously reserved for the future. One of those things was the Pilates mat that sat in my closet for the last ten years. I've always imagined that, in the future, I'll exercise each morning after my relaxing kitchen Bible time. I'm not one of those intense cardio people by any means. I'm more of the "Let's all take deep breaths and stretch" type. And I really have no desire to know what I look like working out, but in my head, I'm graceful and in perfect form, of course.

I pulled out my Pilates mat with both of my boys jumping excitedly. They naturally assumed it was a wrestling mat. While I scrolled through YouTube to find a Pilates teacher who wasn't too obnoxiously perfect, they rolled, pounced, and wrestled all over my mat that hadn't seen the light of day in years. Once I finally settled on a series with a teacher who was just the right amount of sarcastic and calming for my preference, I told the boys I was going to be exercising and they could join in if they liked on blankets behind me. I'd like to say that I was completely calm and full of that Zen feeling everyone tries to reach when I finished my workout routine that day, but I'd be lying.

As soon as I pressed "play" on the remote, my children began to argue. They argued about who was in front of whom, why they couldn't fit themselves on my mat, and eventually, the feet and fists began to fly. But I continued on. At first, I began to speak sternly (but quietly because stretching is for *calm* people) in between poses.

By the end of the 23-minute routine, the boys' fighting had dissipated, and I lay on the mat breathing deeply—proud that I had ignored the many temptations to put the mat back in the closet, whine at my children that they ruined my quest for calm, and give up. I did feel a sense of peace and connection to God, and that's all I was really hoping for anyway. Sometimes the things we save for the future are more beneficial to us now even if they won't look the way we are dreaming about. God wants to connect with us now. He doesn't want to wait 20 years.

When we lean on Christ first to fulfill our greatest relational need—our need to be in relationship with Him—we will see our desperation and neediness for others begin to fade. It won't disappear because we are meant to live in close relationship with others, but the internal void we have that other humans are unable to fill will no longer be there. Only God can truly satisfy our souls.

Reflection Questions

1. Who comprises your community right now? Does it look the way you would like?

2. Have you asked God for friendships? If not, what holds you back?

3. What steps can you take to strengthen your community and friendships right now?

Talk to Him About It

Father, friendship is a tender spot in my heart. Life at home, while filled with blessings, can also feel lonely and isolating. Help me to gain courage in this area, Lord. Let me be the friend I seek, and remind me to reach out to the people You place in my path. When I feel lonely, let me turn to You first, Father, for companionship. I trust You, Lord. Amen.

The New Friend in the Mirror

Embracing Who You Have Become

*If anyone is in Christ, the new creation has
come: The old has gone, the new is here!*
2 Corinthians 5:17

think I need to consider reapplying for some of those work-from-home jobs," I told Ed one night on the way home from a trip. "Maybe I can try for the online teaching positions again. Those stay open throughout the school year," I continued.

Ed stared at the taillights of the car ahead of us and agreed it was probably a good idea. I could tell he was wary that I might once again get too wrapped up in finding a job instead of trusting God.

We were beginning to feel the strain of being a one-income household, and each month felt like a delicate balancing act. One unexpected expense could set us back exponentially, and I regularly worried about our financial stability. I grew up in a family that lived ᵣˌycheck to paycheck. Both of my parents worked hard and still struggled to make ends meet. The lifestyle I now lived—with only one of us bringing home a paycheck—felt reckless and irresponsible despite knowing that God had called me to be home. And even though I no longer felt desperate to find my sense of worth through work, I knew that if I found a job of some sort, it would be helpful to our family.

This time the shift in my thought process was real. I was no longer desperate or needy. Pregnant with our second son, Bradley, I was at peace with my life at home. I looked forward to my life with two sons to care for, and I felt a joyful anticipation that was once nowhere to be found. My life had settled into a comfortable routine. A new normal had been born along with a new me—and I loved it. My days were filled with story times at our local library, sticky kisses, and stacking blocks. Peace had settled in my soul. Christ was with me, in me, and had worked through me to bring me to this place that once seemed foreign. Even impossible.

I was a different person now, no longer looking anywhere but to Christ for approval. When we returned home that evening, I prayed that God would provide me with a job—but only if it were His will. I didn't want it otherwise. I no longer had any interest in being somewhere He didn't want me to be. I went to sleep that night with confident faith that He would answer my prayer one way or another, and I was truly at peace with either answer. We would be taken care of. My God cared about my details, and He knew what we needed.

The next morning, as I opened my laptop to reapply for the teaching job, a voice mail message flashed on my cell phone. I listened to it in complete disbelief. It was the principal of the original school I had applied to: If I were still interested in the teaching position, they were offering an interview. It took me a moment to comprehend what was actually happening. Tears filled my eyes at the thought of such an undeniable display of God's intimate awareness of my details. Slack-jawed at God's merciful provision, I returned the call to the principal and interviewed for the job the next day.

I began working as a telecommuting teacher the following week, teaching a classroom of students from my home—something I once was desperate to do in order to fulfill my own sense of worth. This time, however, the job provided a much-needed boost to our family finances, and I felt secure in who I was—and whose I was. God had truly performed a miracle within me. To this day I am still in awe of the answered prayer with a twenty-four-hour turnaround. How gracious God is to us when we humble ourselves to His will and put our confidence in Him.

Not only did God use this answered prayer to provide relief for my family's financial struggle, but He also used it to give us a deepened and more rock-solid faith. When life gets difficult—as it has a tendency to do—I call on the memory of this answered prayer for reassurance. This is only one of the many times the Lord has performed a work of obvious love on my behalf. He knows me, and He knows what I need. His Word is true. We truly are worth more than the sparrows to God. He will take care of our needs. Where have you seen His unmistakable hand in your life?

When we let go of control and let Jesus direct our steps, suddenly things in life begin to make more sense. Life won't be easy or painless—but it will be right, and the peace that follows is worth it. When we rest in His will we no longer need to fear making a mistake, for we are covered in His grace and mercy. He is the Light that leads us on the unique path He has set before us. We can trust Him.

After Bradley was born, I resigned from my teaching job again. The differences between my resignation after Bryce's birth and Bradley's were staggering. This time I felt no grief, no doubt, and no loss of identity. I knew whose I was, and I knew that what I did had no bearing on my worth. I happily returned to my life, now with two sons to love, and I marveled at the endless gift of grace I had been given.

When we fully embrace the life we've been given—not the one we imagined, the one we used to have, or the one we wish we had—we open the door and invite peace into our lives and hearts. We allow blessings to flow in and out of our lives, living with open hands and hearts, in full surrender to what God will give and take. We trust that He works good in our lives even when we can't see it. This openhanded way of life is the by-product of trust in a good God. There's no longer a compulsion to hold accomplishments and titles in the clenched fist of pride. We are free.

This, of course, doesn't mean we will remain in a constant state of joy. (How I wish it were so—and one day it will be!) There will always be room for improvement. I often long to find a way to stay on top of the never-ending baskets of laundry that line my bedroom—and as I write this, four basketfuls wait to be put away. This is life. It's messy, and no Instagram filter can make a pile of laundry look less daunting. But—thank You, Jesus!—that's not where our focus is meant to be.

Acknowledging Your Growth

Abiding in Christ's gift of peace can be difficult. It took me two years to come to a place of being comfortable in my own skin. They were gut-wrenching, difficult years, spent fighting an exhausting fight between my own will and God's for my life. It's tempting to imagine that Jesus grows impatient with us as we stumble along our path in darkness, looking to Him for guidance only when we are at the end of our own strength. But our imagination is often a dangerous place to be: *Angry* and *impatient* are not accurate descriptions of Christ. Unconditionally loving, a Savior with a servant's heart, Jesus is waiting for the moment when we turn our eyes and hearts to Him at the same time and wait for Him to move us forward, wherever that may be.

When our hearts have been changed, the Holy Spirit will give us opportunities to see our growth and to respond with praise. Last summer, I stood in a Target checkout line behind a former teaching colleague. As the cashier totaled up the many school supplies in her cart, she listened to my friend explain that she was a teacher and then praised her for doing such important work. As the interaction took place, I silently took an inventory of my emotional status.

Where jealousy once would have risen, contentment now rested. Not that long ago, grief would have taken main stage, dimming the brightness of the blessings in my life. Not anymore. I looked at my two little boys and reflected on the undeniable gift of time spent with them without the demands of a career outside of the home. I could only thank God for the new heart He had crafted within me over the last few years.

In the Bible, God makes it very clear that He is detail-oriented. We see His incredibly specific blueprints for the ark, and we marvel at the way He constructed the human body. God is also familiar with the most intricate details that make up our lives and our world. We see this in the book of Luke, when Jesus healed a woman whose back was so horribly bent that she could not stand straight. When Jesus was met with criticism for healing on the Sabbath, He replied, "This dear woman, a daughter of Abraham, has been held in bondage by Satan for eighteen years. Isn't it right that she be released, even on the Sabbath?" (Luke 13:16 NLT). Jesus knew the exact length of time the woman had suffered. He was well acquainted with the details of her life, and He is the same now as He was then. That means He knows your life and your struggles too.

In the Gospel of John, Jesus meets a Samaritan woman at a well. The interaction between Jesus and the woman is interesting on its own, but what caught my attention the last time I read it was the way Jesus used His knowledge of her personal details to display His glory. Jesus asked the woman to get her husband, to which she replied that she had no husband. Jesus' response would make even the most self-assured of us shuffle our feet and drop our jaw in wonder: "You are right when you say you have no husband. The fact is, you have had five husbands, and the man you now have is not your husband. What you have just said is quite true" (John 4:17-18).

Jesus could have told the woman that He knew she's had more than one husband or many, but He didn't. He could have left out the part about her current live-in boyfriend, but He didn't. He used the exact number of men she'd married and went on to mention her current situation as well. We should note that Jesus did not use details to shame the woman, but to increase her faith and cement her belief in Him. She left her conversation with the Savior of the world and shared with her village the story of their meeting: "He told me everything I ever did" (v. 30). The fact that Jesus knew her details mattered to her, and it mattered to those who heard her story.

Jesus stayed to teach in her village a few days after the well encounter, and many came to faith as a result: "They said to the woman, 'We no longer believe just because of what you said; now we have heard for ourselves, and we know that this man really is the Savior of the world'" (v. 42). Her words were not the only reason they believed, but those words opened the door to faith for those people she knew. They believed because of someone else's experience. For the benefit of others, Jesus uses our testimony about His knowledge of our personal details. The gift of knowing Jesus personally is not for us to keep to ourselves. We are to tell others. We are to run back to our own villages and share about the One who knows everything we've ever done.

Have you ever been left in awe of God's knowledge of the details of your life? I imagine that He must smile each time we come face-to-face with the reality of His specific knowledge of us, much like we parents smile when we give our children a special gift we know they'll love.

Jesus' attention to detail does more than provide a foundation for faith. It also reassures us of His kindness and love. As mothers, we often think there's no one who could love our children more than we do. Mentally, we know that God loves them even more than we do, but it's difficult to imagine. In the book of Luke, God gives us moms a special message about the way He cares for our children and for us. In the story, a synagogue leader's young daughter was dying, and he begged Jesus to come to his home. I've read this account many times never noticing how Jesus' attention to detail is on full display.

Jesus arrived at the man's home and called Peter, James, and John to go into the room with Him, the synagogue leader, and his wife. Jesus raised the girl from the dead, but He didn't stop there: "Her spirit returned, and at once she stood up. Then Jesus told [her parents] to give her something to eat" (Luke 8:55). Jesus cared so much about the little girl that after raising her from the dead He wanted to make sure she ate. Her parents stood in awe and wonder, and Jesus' concern was that she was hungry. There's something so moving to me about this detail in Scripture—that the God of the universe would love so completely each one of us as well as our children. The degree to which He cares about our personal needs and intricacies is astonishing. It shouldn't be! After all, the Bible tells us He knows the number of hairs on our scalps and the total days in our lifetimes, yet it is in this simplest request of Jesus that I see this truth of God's care become a tangible reality.

Perhaps you, too, sometimes struggle with the knowledge that God knows the smallest specifics of your life. You find it difficult to trust that He sees the way you long for healing—emotional, physical, or otherwise. Maybe you yearn for another child, or you worry that you're not the right mother for the ones you have. I assure you, God sees you, He hears you, and He knows you in a way that no one on this earth ever could.

Jesus knew that the morning after I prayed about our financial situation and my desire to find work, He would line up an interview I had desperately sought months earlier. Your details are just as known to Him. He is so intricately familiar with our lives and every breath we take, there is simply no need to be anxious. As someone who struggles with anxiety, I don't say that casually. To be honest, after the adrenaline from an encounter with Jesus fades, my humanity—like a grocery cart with a bum wheel that keeps trying to turn left (why do I always pick those?)—wants to veer back to an anxious way of living. I must make a conscious decision to place my trust in God and leave behind the anxious thoughts. It's not easy, and it's a struggle most days. There's always something to be worried about if you're paying attention to the world instead of to the God who made it.

Worry isn't the way of Christ, though, and if we are in Him and He is in us, this worry isn't our way either. Jesus wants more for us than we want for ourselves. He sees what our lives could be if we lived in complete faith; He sees the possibilities that await us on the other side of half-hearted belief. Christ Himself lived a life of complete faith in and unity with the Father. Jesus knows how sweet it is to live and move in unhindered surrender even if it costs. It's a place He wants us to go not just from time to time, but to stay. What would life look like if even on the worst days, we sat cradled in the peace of the Father's arms? Our lives would be full of His peace, the peace He died to give us. There's no way to overestimate the Father's level of love and concern for us. He loves us in a way that is simply unfathomable to our mortal minds.

What would life look like if even on the worst days, we sat cradled in the peace of the Father's arms?

When we embrace the new creation we've become, our old habits and the false beliefs we held about God and ourselves become unfamiliar. Our new normal and our renewed purpose take center stage in our lives, and the resulting sense of peace reverberates through our families. The loss of a work family and a set schedule no longer breeds unspoken frustration or anger in your life. Friends who have drifted away are let go with an honest blessing. If God pruned them from your life, you now accept that He must know something you don't. You see everything through different lenses, and a sense of gratitude has replaced the negative emotions you once experienced. Others who have witnessed this rebirth may acknowledge the growth they've seen in you, and those who haven't been in contact with you for a while may feel like they don't know you anymore.

You are no longer who you were, and while this growth is a beautiful act of God's work in your life, it might be unsettling to others. Sometimes happiness is not shared, and jealousy takes root instead. As I mentioned earlier, the judgments of others about you are not your concern. Those people who might be stifling the work of Christ in your life, even without knowing it, will most likely be the ones who reject or scoff at the new person you've become. When it is tempting to question whether who you are now is "too much" or if it's all been worth it, remember that standing closer to God is always the right place to be. This new place that God has lifted you to is in stark contrast to where you began—as it should be.

During a recent visit to see my obstetrician for an annual checkup I was placed in an exam room that held more memories than I could count. The small beige room is decorated with pictures of mother and baby animals embracing. I glanced up from the table I sat on to see the familiar drawing of a mother giraffe kissing the top of her baby's head. As I studied the image, as I've done countless times before, I was met with reminders of all of the other women I had been when I sat on the edge of that table, legs crossed and paper gown rough against my skin, in that very room.

There was the newly married woman—wracked with nerves and anticipation, feeling too young to really consider mother-hood, but knowing she wasn't—inquiring about her ability to bear a child. There was also the woman, pregnant and terrified, who lay on the table with her husband at her side as she witnessed with awe the beating of her five-week-old baby's heart. In that moment she glimpsed the power of God within her. There were all the moments she sat on the edge, literally and figuratively, belly growing larger by the week, counting down the days to meeting her son—and herself.

I wandered down the hallway of my mind to the next season of visits in that room. This time the woman sat on the same table, peering down at the newborn in a carrier next to her instead of at the pictures above her. He was tiny and wrinkled, and her body felt like the forgotten box of a cherished present on Christmas morning: torn, empty, and unrecognizable from only moments before. Her sock-covered feet dangled beneath her as she prayed he wouldn't cry to nurse one more time. She was anxious to rush through the appointment where she would fight the tears as she told the doctor how exhausted she was—and that maybe she was depressed. I can hardly keep the tears from escaping as I write these words about the glorious but painful transitions I've traveled through by the grace of God.

Who knew that once we took the leap into motherhood, the adventure would feel more like a crawl in some moments and like flying in others? The best of us can hardly keep track of the ups and downs this path takes. The seasons God has led me through, gently and faithfully, have blurred into a life, and I've become the version of the woman I am now. I'm still becoming, every day, and so are you.

> *I'm still becoming, every day,*
> *and so are you.*

Without much fanfare, life happens, and before we know it, we are sitting on a table, in a paper gown, staring at a giraffe portrait and remembering who we once were. Your journey will look different from mine, no question, but I am confident that you have done quite the traveling to get where you are. I encourage you to take a few moments and identify the milestones marking the path that you have followed to this place with God. As you wander down the hallways of your own mind, can you pinpoint some specific moments before things changed? Perhaps it was before you walked down the aisle to marry or before you met your baby for the first time. When you recall who you were during that time, you can surely see a difference between the woman then and the woman you are now.

How did God walk beside you during those moments of transition? Was His presence obvious, or was it a gentle whisper to your soul that you weren't alone? Allow yourself some time to sit in quiet reflection with God about your journey to being the woman you are today. He has never left your side, and it is incredibly faith building to identify the places where He held you close and then to thank Him for His faithfulness.

Owning Your Growth

God is a redeeming God, and He lifts His children out of valleys (some deeper than others) time and again. It is not the job of friends and family to understand God's will for your life, nor is it your job to make them understand. The only praise and affirmation you seek comes from Him alone. Let the approval of others come whenever it may happen—and it may never come. Right after I submitted my resignation, it seemed like everywhere I went, I saw friends from work. When I'd be looking worn-out, hair up in a ponytail, and frantically pushing my cart through the store to avoid a meltdown due to an impending nap-time, I would run into another work friend. "It's so great you can take this time off," she would begin.

We'd make small talk for a little while, and usually I was internally praying that the snacks I was frantically feeding Bryce, one after another, would keep him happy. I always foresaw the inevitable question: "So when are you coming back to work? When Bryce is in school, or…" and their voice would trail off. Back then, I said I planned to return once he entered kindergarten, but even as the words left my mouth, I knew that though the plan sounded good, it didn't feel like the path I was to take. My answer was just what those I was speaking to expected to hear because they knew me as someone passionate about my work and my students. It's so difficult to speak our truth to those who knew us before, isn't it? Before a resignation, before a child, before an internal shift shattered and resettled our lives more beautifully than we could dream.

Internally, I thought about the next child I knew we wanted to have, and my mind reeled with what life would look like then or even a year or two from the place where I stood. I left those conversations frustrated not because of the questions asked, but because I didn't believe my own answers. Why couldn't I answer a friend—or myself—honestly?

Many of us who have chosen to be home with our children face questions about the future, and they feel daunting even if they come from within. *When will we return to work? Do we plan to have more children? What about our education? Did we work so hard just to let it go to waste? Who will watch the kids if we do go back to work? Do we really want to miss out on the moments with our children we have the privilege of enjoying now? What kind of mom would give that up?* The questions feel like judgment wrapped in innocent curiosity, and our knee-jerk responses are often not the best ones to offer when other people are the ones asking. Those asking mean no harm (at least I prefer to believe they don't). It's our internal dialogue that places judgment where there is none to be found. We are, in fact, our worst enemies.

When we find ourselves judging ourselves, it's most important to remember where we've been and where we're going. We are not meant to stay in the valley, and there is no shame in standing tall on the mountaintop and declaring God's grace that carried you there. Instead of shuffling around your words when someone asks a question, refuse to accept the guilt that whispers lies. Speak of your newfound contentment at home, for there is no reason to be ashamed of the gifts of God. Regardless of the questions or judgments of others, we know that our worth and our future reside with Christ. We have come much too far to allow the simple curiosities of others to shake the foundation of our faith in the path God has placed before us. When the questions come from within and you find yourself in the endless "What if" or "What will I do then" cycle, take stock of the ways Jesus has been faithful to lead you and provide for you along the road you've been walking.

One of the many gifts of knowing that my worth is firmly placed in Jesus is when I am now asked questions about the future, I am able to respond with confidence and believe my own words. I'm comfortable telling others that I don't know when I'll return to work and that I'm homeschooling my now kindergarten-age son. I'm fully comfortable sharing that I plan to keep homeschooling as long as it makes sense for our family—and, I explain, when—if ever—it makes sense for me to return to the classroom, I'll reenter the working world then.

This mind-set is a far cry from the old me, the one who—because of the constant feeling of being left out, left behind, and less than—dreaded the social media pictures of beautifully decorated classrooms ready for a new school year posted by teacher friends. Yet when we examine the distance we've traveled once we've made it to the other side of our grief, loss, and misplaced identity, we actually see just how far Jesus Himself has carried us—and gratitude is the appropriate heartfelt response.

Embrace who you are now as well as the woman you're becoming who has been waiting in the wings all along. She's vibrant and faithful. She's confident not because of her own abilities, but because of God's power through her. She's calm and content: She knows her future rests in the arms of Jesus and that He's so worthy of her trust. She's grateful for the past that has led to the present: The schooling, the effort, and the career that have brought her to this place offer unique gifts that now benefit her life and her children. When doubt rears its head, as it is known to do, this woman can look it in the eye and meet its lies with the truth. She is not what she produces; she is a daughter of the holy God of the universe. Her worth far exceeds any work she could ever do. Can you feel the change within? Walk forward confident in the grace and mercy God has covered you with. This is the continuation of His miraculous work within you.

> *You are not what you produce; you are a daughter of the holy God of the universe.*

The woman you've become through this difficult transitional experience is who you are meant to be at this moment. Note that I didn't say that it is who you're meant to be—period. We are always growing into clearer reflections of Christ as we follow His will and pursue lives that honor Him. Until He calls us home, we are all works in progress.

The blessing of this journey is not only that you are becoming closer to the image of Christ, but also that you have more to give to your precious children. You are offering your cherished loved ones a more fulfilled mother who finds her joy and her life in Christ. It's the greatest gift that we as mothers can offer our children: to know God and to reflect His love in their lives from an early age. You're doing this thing well, friend. Keep going.

Reflection Questions

1. When, if ever, has God left you speechless by revealing His intimate knowledge of your life?

2. As you reflect on your journey to becoming the woman you are today, what are you grateful for?

3. When questioned about your life at home, do you answer with confidence? If not, why do you think that is?

⤳ Talk to Him About It

Lord, with constant love and grace, You have brought me to this place in life. I am so grateful. I ask that You would strengthen me now, to embrace all You have made me to be. Remind me of every way You have held me up in my weakness and allowed me to overcome struggle through Your power and presence with me. You are so good to me, Father. I trust You. Amen.

The Beauty and the Balance

Living in the Fullness God Intended

Beware the barrenness of a busy life.
Socrates

My kids have this board game called Aladdin's Flying Carpet Game that they love to play with Ed and me. It's actually really fun to play, and it's one we can all enjoy. (There aren't many games marketed to kids I enjoy these days!) That game has a small plastic magic carpet, suspended in the air by a plastic wand that holds a magnet, making the carpet look to be floating in midair. To play, each person takes a turn choosing various plastic pieces from a bag to load onto the carpet. If it becomes overloaded, even by one seemingly light piece, the carpet will crash, and the game ends—usually with much crying and possibly screaming, but perhaps this only happens in my home.

Our lives are no different from the Magic Carpet. If we don't carefully choose the things that fill our lives, there's bound to be a crash—and it won't be pretty. Whether the expenditures are emotional, physical, or spiritual, we are only made to do so much. Finding a healthy balance and actually keeping it is key to living a life of fulfillment and joy.

We live in a society that values to a fault the word *busy*. We fill up our schedules and those of our children with activities that may keep us and them busy—but at what cost? Because of an ever-increasing demand by parents to keep their little ones always on the go, there is a wide assortment of activities to choose from. Soccer, gymnastics, dance, martial arts, football, cheerleading—the list goes on. Between church, school, homework, playtime, and extracurricular activities, I think it's fair to say we all suffer from an overload of activity. The worst part is, during our downtime we spend our precious minutes reading the news or on social media, neither of which is particularly relaxing or life-giving.

The beauty of finding and keeping balance is that you'll never give so much of yourself that you feel depleted, and you won't take so much you feel guilty. Sometimes the balance will slip—the corner of your carpet will begin to come perilously close to a crash—but you'll be able to rearrange the things in your life to prevent it. In order to keep yourself from crashing, however, you'll need to know how to rearrange it the right way.

Only you will know how to schedule your daily life to meet the needs of your family. Sitting down together to talk about what you value as a family is an important first step, and it will help to put everyone on the same page (especially valuable when it comes time to remove things). Listening to each other is vital in deciding how to move forward, and the simple act of hearing one another out (even if the idea or suggestion is crazy) will help you avoid bitterness and resentment in the long run. Knowing what you need and how to communicate it is an incredibly important skill.

In the early days of staying home, I found myself too frustrated to offer Ed any real suggestions about what I needed from him. The problem wasn't just that I was feeling depressed about all of the changes happening, but also that I was overwhelmed. I didn't know what I needed; I only knew it looked different from what I had. Instead of taking the time to express my underlying irritation, I grew bitter and resentful. Learn from my mistakes: Don't punish your family for not knowing your unmet needs.

If you need your spouse to give you time on the weekends to be alone, then ask for it. One of the biggest revelations I had when I thought about what I really needed was the realization that I needed weekends to look different from the weekdays. Throughout this book, I've discussed the monotony of staying home with children every day, and I cannot stress enough the value of making sure your weekends look different from your weekdays in some significant ways.

This doesn't mean that you have to have a getaway every weekend or even once every month. But I found in my own life, it is important to do something (anything!) that looks different from Monday through Friday on the two days my husband is home with us. Sometimes that's doing something as a family that I'm not brave enough to do alone during the week with the boys, or it could be something that I know we would all enjoy more together. Sometimes it's getting out of the house alone to write or staying home while Ed takes the kids out for something fun.

Is there anything better than *You've Got Mail* on repeat with chocolate and a laptop in front of you? There isn't for me. Whatever it is, if you need a change, then speak up about it and identify the reasons why it's so important. I explained it to Ed by saying that for me, being home with the kids on the weekend feels as though I never leave my office. I need a change of pace to recharge and refresh myself for the coming week.

Changing up the weekend might be difficult for some people because perhaps your spouse is already out of the home much of the time and wants to spend weekends there for a change. If this is the case, you might want to consider taking at least a few hours to yourself each weekend to go and do something you enjoy, even if it's by yourself. You need the time to recharge in order to be the mom God has called you to be to your children—so don't for one second feel an ounce of guilt. Your husband needs a respite from his office space, and you do too.

During the week balance for me looks like waking each day, readying myself (I'm a makeup girl, and now that I don't have an infant in the home, I make time for it), serving my boys breakfast, and then taking 15 minutes to eat my own. While I drink my coffee, I usually read the Bible or a devotional. For a long time I skipped that last step. Spending time with Jesus was not always a priority. I'd fit Him in when I felt low or received some bad news. It was basically a self-written prescription of Jesus as needed—the result of my being unaware of what (of who!) I was missing.

My mornings once began with coffee and social media—not exactly the most spiritually nourishing way to start a day energized to be the best mother possible to my boys. I now know better than to attempt to begin my day without some sort of time spent with the Lord. Some mornings the time with Him might be shorter than others, but I know that I'll also be in consistent communication with Him throughout the day as I pray for patience—and that there's still ice cream in the freezer. Starting my day with Jesus is absolutely necessary to put everything in perspective, and it puts Him first in my day both literally and spiritually.

Some mornings I have toy monster trucks flying by my face as I read and pray, but I've mastered the art of tuning in to God and tuning out everything else. The boys call this my "Jesus Time," and they see me make time for the Lord every single day. Sometimes they'll join me with their own Bibles, and we share a sweet time together with God. Other times are a bit more chaotic and less serene. I once almost lost an eye to Batman's foot while reading God's Word. Many mornings end with me closing my Bible too early with a sigh and a quick prayer that consists of "You know I tried, Lord." I imagine He chuckles at the scenes playing out in my living room and kitchen on a daily basis.

Don't feel like a failure if your life does not allow for an hour of uninterrupted time with Christ each morning. (As I said earlier, I dream of one day having unending time to study the Bible.) I know we are often told to wake an hour earlier than our children to set an hour aside for God. I have done this a time or two and find it to be wonderful. I also know that we are exhausted as it is, and if we make time with God a chore, we are less likely to do it.

I would also hate for my boys to never see me starting my day with God. Our kids need to see us model a life of faith, and if they are sleeping while we receive holy fuel for our days, how will they know what some practical steps in a faithful life look like? Not only that, but God looks at our hearts. When we set our alarms early and resentfully open a devotional or our Bibles to spend time reading His Word through swollen eyes yearning for sleep, we are not in the mind-set or heart position before the Lord that we need to be.

In other words, we don't need to make God a requirement that we resent. Imagine meeting a friend at Starbucks, and she appears at your table half-awake, slumped in her chair, and sighing heavily about being there. It probably wouldn't feel as though she truly wanted to spend time with you, right? So if you can do it, starting the day with God is important—but don't force yourself into compliance.

Balance in Everyday Life

For you, balance might look like reading the Bible on an app while you wait in a carpool lane. Perhaps you listen to God's Word while you drive or get ready in the morning. There are so many ways to start our day with the Father. You can also pray and ask Jesus how He would like to meet you each day. How would He prefer to spend time with you? Ask Him to show you where and how to fit in the maximum amount of time with Him daily. He loves to spend time with us, and He will be faithful to answer. We do what we can, and we leave the rest to Him.

What about the rest of the day? What does balance look like in the four billion other minutes until bedtime? Every day I try to play with my boys and meet their needs. (How many snacks can one mom provide in a day? I'm positive I beat my personal record daily!) And every day I try to carve out some time to feed my own soul—whether that is through exercise, writing, or reading. Writing and reading feed my soul in ways that are long-lasting, and I know that if I can get in even ten minutes of reading an interesting book, that time is worth it for my well-being and attitude. Another self-care practice I've taken up is drinking herbal tea. I have found that I love researching herbal teas and trying new ones each week. It's a simple way to slow down every day and feel as though I'm doing something for myself.

God has such a sense of humor. When I received the news that this book was going to be a published reality, I was smack-dab in the middle of living out balance. I was sitting cross-legged on a stuffed elephant pillow-chair, playing superheroes with Bradley. I found it perfectly fitting that I was impersonating the Joker and ducking imaginary Spider-Man-created webs when I was told about this dream of mine coming to fruition. Isn't that just like God?

In the pain of losing a beloved career, I learned to dream again. I rediscovered what it was that made my pulse quicken—and had done so all my life. God removed from my eyes the scales that I never knew existed, and He showed me what He had for me in this new season of walking with Him. He is so very good, sisters. He will do the exact same for you. Half the battle is learning what He has placed in you that finally has a chance to bloom. Discovering balance means finding ways to incorporate into your daily life things you enjoy, and doing so is necessary not just for you, but also for your entire family. Believe me, they *need* you to be living out your purpose.

> *Discovering balance means finding ways to incorporate into your daily life things you enjoy.*

It's tempting to play the martyr, isn't it? To give of yourself unceasingly until bitter and sarcastic responses to your husband asking about your day become second nature. I know the temptation to martyrdom all too well. But giving up on living your life in a way you enjoy isn't fair to yourself or to your family.

These words might sound a bit like tough love here because it is. No one is going to be able to tell you how to live this life. No one will be able to help you find that inner God-spark that lights up your world and spurs you on to find more and more light and then share it with others. This is it—this is your life—and it's meant to be enjoyed and lived to the full.

Your children won't know what will bring you joy (in addition to them, of course), and they aren't meant to. They also won't know that you need to care for yourself, and they surely won't give you the time to do so. That's why you need to take it. Do the things that matter to you not as an act of selfishness, but because it's what living well looks like. It's also what your kids need you to do; they just don't know it. Mothers aren't meant to be martyrs.

When Bryce was a newborn, he only wanted me. I'd hand him to some well-meaning relative who asked to hold him, and after a few moments, he would wail to be back in my arms. Then, peacefully nestled into my chest, he would fall back to sleep. Secretly, I loved it. I loved knowing that I had what Bryce needed to feel secure in this world and that I was the only one who could provide it. As Bryce and Bradley have grown older and we've left well behind us the newborn baby stage, that feeling of being able to provide everything they need has begun to fade as well. I'm well aware that I cannot be all that they need forever. Only God can do that, and it's been that way from the beginning. The truth is, though, it's not that I feel less equipped; it's that I sometimes slip into the feeling that out there somewhere there's a better mom for them. She's quiet, she's never short with them, and she never ever raises her voice. She never curses or makes threats she knows she'll never act on.

It's really easy to believe these lies especially when I'm not taking the time for the little things I enjoy that make a big difference in my heart and soul. In reality, there is no better mom for my boys. Just like their newborn selves, they still only want me. I'm positive it's the same with your children.

You are the best mom for your children because you're theirs. The little hands that clutch yours to cross the street won't ever want to hold another mother's hand. The one they hold has been the touch they've known since their first breath. It has rubbed their back in the dark of night, rested cool against their forehead when they were sick, and massaged growing pains into nonexistence. They know that you are the only one they would ever choose—and it's vital that you know this in the deepest place of your heart too. You are the only mother for these children, and you need to take the best care of yourself to be the best for them.

You need to take care of yourself to be the best version of you for your kids.

For you, the balanced life will look different than it does for me because we are all beautifully unique. The one thing that will be the same is your need for Jesus every day. We cannot be whole and fulfilled without Him. The rest of your plan for balance is up to you. As stay-at-home mothers, we have so many choices—and we can be grateful for the opportunity to become exactly who God is calling us to be.

As our children grow and change, so do the needs and preferences of our family. I hope you, your husband, and your (older) kids have made a commitment to grow together and to give each other plenty of grace through the family's inevitable transitions.

At the beginning of this journey of stay-at-home motherhood, I struggled immensely. Clearly, my struggle is what birthed the book you're now reading—that should tell you that not only was the struggle real, but it was lengthy! Looking back, I believe much of the pain I experienced was rooted in false beliefs that I wasn't even aware of. Beliefs like I no longer control how my life is lived, I no longer have worth to others unless they need their diaper changed, I'm not brave enough to work and raise a family, and I don't have what it takes to do this mom gig. Sound familiar? The transformative work of Christ in my life is, in a word, miraculous. The life I lead now is one I fiercely love—and that's a long way from where I started.

My prayer is that as you've read each chapter, you have also been able to call out these false beliefs and replace them with the truth: You are a beloved daughter of Christ. You do have a choice in the way you live your life. In fact, you have more choices than many other people, and your ability to choose is an enormous blessing even though it comes with its own difficulties, to be sure. Your worth in Christ far surpasses any professional title, and your worth is not earned. It is a gift from God. You can do all things through Christ—and if He had called you to work outside of the home while raising your children, you would have been able to. You do have what it takes because you have Him. He has simply taken you on a detour. This change in your path is full of life lessons to be learned, rough edges to be smoothed, and lives to be conformed more to His image.

On many days this life at home isn't easy, but the moments when being at home is worth it far outnumber and outweigh any hardships. And nestled beneath your hatred of high-pitched cartoon voiceovers, and your deep love of that first sip of coffee in the morning, is heart knowledge you might never have expected to gain. This season at home is the gift of a lifetime, and you are already abundantly equipped to receive it.

Blooming When It's Time

Last summer we planted beautiful perennial flowers. When we placed them in the ground, they were vibrant pinks and purples—a gorgeous example of what God intended flowers to be. When the blooms disappeared from the plants in autumn, leaving bare stems and leaves, Bryce noticed and grew concerned.

"Did they die, Mom?" he asked with sadness in his voice.

"No, they're okay. They're just waiting for the right time to bloom again," I replied.

We aren't so different, are we? Wait no more, sweet friends. Your time has come.

Reflection Questions

1. Between waking up and bedtime, what does balance look like for you? What pockets of time are built in for things you enjoy?

2. How can you fit time with God into your day?

3. How will you bloom?

Talk to Him About It

Father, thank You for this journey You have taken me on. Help me move forward now in confidence of who I am in You. It is only in You that I find my identity and worth. I'm so honored to be Your daughter. My whole heart is Yours, Lord. Amen.

Notes

1. Chapter 4: Netflix and Pajamas
   Margery Williams, *The Velveteen Rabbit* (New York: Doubleday, 2014), 20.

2. Chapter 5: Good Grief
   Anne Roiphe, *Epilogue: A Memoir* (New York: HarperCollins, 2008), 4.

3. Chapter 6: More Than Motherhood
   St. Catherine of Siena, quoted in *Setting the World on Fire: The Brief, Astonishing Life of St. Catherine of Siena,* by Shelley Emling (New York: St. Martin's Press, 2016), xvii.

4. Chapter 8: Making Friends with Telemarketers
   Paul Tillich, "Let Us Dare to Have Solitude," *Union Seminary Quarterly Review,* May 1957, 9-11, 13.

Acknowledgments

To...

Ed, my husband, best friend, and cheerleader in all things—you've seen me at my worst, and you've stayed by my side, loving me back to my best. Thank you, honey. I love you with all I've got.

Bryce and Bradley—your dad and I love you both beyond words. You have been the sweetest detour of my life.

My parents, Larry and Carrie Nyquist—I love you, and I'm so proud to be your daughter. Thank you for believing in me.

Zach and Berenice Nyquist—thank you for cheering me on, it's meant so much. I love you both!

My mother-in-law, Rosik Datyalian—thank you for being such a blessing in our lives. We love you.

Nikki Echabarne—thank you for your friendship and prayers. You are a gift.

Sherry Lewis—thank you for always being there, and willing to get frozen yogurt.

Kathleen Nyquist—thank you for being a source of endless encouragement on this journey.

Patty Nyquist—thank you for...everything.

The rest of the Nyquist family—I love you all. Thank you for cheering me on.

My literary agent, Rachelle Gardner, of Books & Such Literary Management—your wisdom and guidance throughout this process have been invaluable. I'm so grateful you're in my corner!

My editor, Kathleen Kerr—I had no idea the editing process could be so fun! Thank you for your hilarious manuscript comments and your incredible wisdom.

The entire team at Harvest House—thank you for making this process so much better than I could ever have imagined.

The moms who make up Sweet Pea Nation—you ladies are the best. Thank you for your support the last seven years. I love you all!

Jesus, my Savior—only You could have orchestrated this. Only You. Words aren't adequate to express my gratitude. You have my heart forever.

About the Author

Jen Babakhan is a writer living in California with her husband, Ed; two sons, Bryce and Bradley; and a stubborn shih tzu named Bailey. After leaving a career in education to stay home with her children, Jen resumed her pursuit of a lifelong love of writing. She is a regular contributor to *Reader's Digest*, and her articles have been featured on MSN and Fox News. She loves coffee ice cream, solo trips to Target, and days spent at the beach. She believes that Jesus is the answer to every problem and wants others to experience His extravagant love firsthand. Visit Jen online at www.JenBabakhan.com. She would love to interact with you on social media. You can find her on Instagram and Twitter, @jenbabakhan, and on Facebook at www.Facebook.com/jenbabakhanauthor.

To learn more about Harvest House books and to read sample chapters, log on to our website:

www.harvesthousepublishers.com

HARVEST HOUSE PUBLISHERS
EUGENE, OREGON